MW01223509

The Road to Resiliency

The Road to Resiliency

Troy Payne

Order this book online at www.trafford.com
or email orders@trafford.com

Most Trafford titles are also available at major online book retailers.

© Copyright 2011 Troy Payne.
All rights reserved. No part of this publication may be reproduced, stored in a retrieval
system, or transmitted, in any form or by any means, electronic, mechanical, photocopying,
recording, or otherwise, without the written prior permission of the author.

"Who Will Cry for the Little Boy?" from FINDING FISH by ANTWONE
QUENTON FISHER and MIM EICHLER RIVAS

COPYRIGHT © 2001 BY ANTWONE QUENTON FISHER AND MIM
EICHLER RIVAS. Reprinted by permission of HarperCollins Publishers

Printed in the United States of America.

ISBN: 978-1-4269-4983-8 (sc)
ISBN: 978-1-4269-4984-5 (hc)
ISBN: 978-1-4269-4985-2 (e)

Library of Congress Control Number: 2010918331

Trafford rev. 02/03/2011

 www.trafford.com

North America & international
toll-free: 1 888 232 4444 (USA & Canada)
phone: 250 383 6864 ♦ fax: 812 355 4082

I dedicate this book to the memory of Dr. Edith H. Grotberg, whose dedication to promoting early childhood development and the human capacity for resilience inspired these pages.

I also dedicate this book to the Universe, may it be an instrument of healing.

CONTENTS

ACKNOWLEDGMENTS

I offer much love to my many brothers and sisters who have shared this journey with me and who have contributed their talents, support, love, and encouragement in the creating of this book. You all hold a special place in my heart, and I am so grateful to have each of you in my life. A BIG thank you to **Lesley Scorgie** for sharing your wisdom and experience in manifesting a book. **David Kalinchuk** – your friendship and contributions mean so much to me; thank you, my friend. **Dr. Lee Burchinal** and **Dr. Judith Paphazy** – thank you for believing in this project and for helping me honor Dr. Edith Grotberg's work. **Rhonda Victoor** – much love to my big sister for your ever-flowing kindness. If everyone in the universe had a heart as big as yours, I would be out of work, but what a beautiful world it would be. **Michelle Kowalchuk** – I will always be grateful to you for your generosity of spirit, your contributions, and for helping me take those last few steps. Thank you all for sharing the vision of encouraging, engaging, and empowering others.

FOREWORD

I was pleased to respond to Troy Payne's request to write this foreword. I know readers will benefit from the redemptive nature of his narrative.

His book tells a harrowing story of childhood abuse. The very people who should have been trustworthy, Kyle's parents, failed badly in their role. Thus, Kyle was exposed to the incompetence and neglect of his mother and the brutality of Frank, his stepfather. Part rescued by his adoptive father, Michael, Kyle's respite was short-lived, as Michael, too, proved to be another incompetent adult.

Adolescence is a set of roller-coaster experiences with adults who sometimes show they care but are unreliable when conflicting interests or needs emerge. Thus drugs, theft and self-destructive behaviors can highlight these uncertain years. However, during these years, there were also some real, trustworthy adults who did not deceive Kyle, e.g., the school counselor, some of his teachers and his grandmother. It is the belief of these adults in Kyle's capacity to be and to do better, plus Kyle's eventual willingness to look at his adversities and subsequent behaviors honestly, that helped him develop the necessary resilient responses. These resilience responses helped free him from his dysfunctional past. They freed him to look for, and find the capacity for good in himself. And they freed him to forgive those who behaved so badly toward him. Of course, Kyle will never forget the terrible abuse he suffered. But as he has forgiven his abusers and deceivers, he has come to understand that he is not the victim of the effects of abuse. He is free to look forward, with optimism and faith, to a productive future. In these behaviors and decisions, Kyle also demonstrates an absolute truth, namely that all behaviors and decisions are choices, and as such invoke consequences.

Troy has dedicated this book to Dr. Edith Henderson Grotberg. Edith was a worldwide authority on the promotion of resilience (http://www.resilnet@uiuc.edu). Her elegant and powerfully effective I HAVE, I AM, I CAN resilience model is successfully used in many countries throughout the world. Edith Henderson Grotberg was my mentor, colleague and above all, dear friend. It is fitting that Troy gives credit to her and the many other people whose works and thoughts have helped Kyle overcome the effects of the shocking adversities to which he was subjected. Through his reading and study he learned to see the world from another perspective, a kinder and more optimistic perspective, a perspective that has enriched his life.

Kyle, having faced, overcome, been strengthened and even transformed by using resilience to deal with his adversities, has decided to dedicate his new life to helping others. I am sure he will be very successful in this wonderful and fulfilling choice.

On Edith's, and indeed my own, behalf: "Well done Troy." I know you will use your learnings and reflections to help promote resilience and well-being in others.

Dr. Judith E Papházy PhD, FACE

PREFACE

Have you ever been moved to tell a story? Storytelling is such a powerful means to inform or inspire others, especially when those stories are true. This book is Kyle's story, a true story - the story of one boy. I could have chosen to tell you the story of any one of the hundreds of youth I've worked with since 1996. That was the year I decided to start creating ripples.

A Ripple's Reach

~by Michelle Lynn Kowalchuk

There is beauty
in the moment…
when we first realize
that we are not
alone

Not drifting in isolation
but rather connected

to universal energy
and all there is

Inspired by the light
known to live
within each of us,
but not always seen,
not always dusted off,
not always given time to uncover
or discover

It is in the moment
when someone sees our light,
we come to understand
how each act of kindness
as simple as a smile
lives on...
in each soul
it touches

One moment given
freely without judgement
or expectation,
forever gives
back to us

A sense of knowing
the peace we create
within another soul that once felt
lost

Adrift on its own
when we open our heart...
willing to look beyond the
surface of another

Never overwhelmed
by a sense of a vastness
we feel cannot change

Knowing instead
with each soul
we touch, we link ourselves
to the next one
and change their story

One breath of kind words
One hand of support
One act of compassion -
One smile

Just one
has the ability
to rejuvenate
to acknowledge
to celebrate

One is enough to create
One difference
One light

that sees...
and illuminates...
and heals
One soul

Creating one ripple

Circular
infinitely expanding
in every direction

It begins with just one -
yet extends forever...
in the lives
of
all

"A Ripple's Reach" is a beautiful poem of the power each one of us has to be able to make a difference in the lives of others. Regardless of how small or grand the gesture, each one of us has the ability to change someone's life. The poem reminds us that every soul is connected. The ripple that we initiate in one person's life expands into the lives of so many others.

During my transition from childhood to adulthood, I knew I needed to create those ripples so I enrolled in college and became a child and youth care worker. While I was attending college, I worked in a variety of counseling, one-on-one tutoring, summer youth programs, and camps.

Upon graduation, I received a position with the provincial government, working in a residential treatment facility for youths. Here I had met youths who had been in and out of care and protective custody their entire lives. Bounced around from home to home, some had endured incredible amounts of mental, physical, or sexual abuse; some cases were a combination of all three. Many of the children seemed to have gotten lost in the system that was designed to protect them. Society's and government's failure to intervene in time or effectively became one of the factors in why many of these children were ending up in juvenile detention centers and/or repeating the lifestyles of abuse and addictions from where they came. After a year at the facility, I decided to return to one-on-one youth and family counseling.

Being one of few men in the field, I received numerous referrals from Alberta Mental Health and Children & Family Services. So many young boys and teenagers were and are in need of positive role models in their lives. Again, these young people had suffered incredible amounts of pain and adversity in their lives.

So there I was, creating "ripples" in a variety of settings for almost ten years. I loved connecting with all those young minds, but I could only help one or two at a time - sometimes a handful - and in situations like the summer camps, I could impact around seventy. It got to a point where helping so few at a time just wasn't good enough for me anymore. I wanted to connect with hundreds or even thousands at a time. This was the birth of Wellness Realization. Over the years, I had given dozens and dozens of classroom presentations to youth, promoting the various youth initiatives I was working on. I felt comfortable talking in front of an audience, and most of all, I had fun doing it! Eight years ago, I decided to take my experiences, knowledge and education as a youth worker, combined with my experiences, knowledge and education of entrepreneurship, and travel the path of self-employment. I developed a number of keynote presentations, specializing in resiliency and cultural diversity. I have been traveling across North America ever since, speaking to youth and adult audiences at conferences and events.

As a youth counselor, I have had the privilege and opportunity of connecting with hundreds of youths. As a professional speaker, I have had the chance to connect with over one hundred thousand people. This book is the culmination of adversities we are all faced with, and it begins with Kyle's story . . .

CHAPTER 1 - Innocence

Sharon and Michael

Sharon looked at Michael, and both looked at the newest addition to their family, eleven month-old Kyle. Kyle had been given up for adoption at birth and placed in an orphanage. Today, Kyle met his new parents, both in their twenties: Sharon, a waitress at a Chinese food restaurant, and Michael, a janitor for the provincial government in Alberta, Canada. They owned one car and a modest bi-level two-bedroom home. With Kyle's adoption, they created what many would describe as the perfect family picture: the modern nuclear family who often entertained their immediate family members with dinners and small gatherings. However, the perfect family picture ends there.

Sharon and Michael fought constantly, resulting in the end of their marriage by the time Kyle reached the age of four. Sharon assumed custody of Kyle and moved into a small two-bedroom apartment, and Michael received visitation every other weekend.

Sharon and Frank

Six short months after the divorce was finalized, Sharon moved in with Frank, a big burly twenty-four year-old man with shoulder-length brown hair and a thick beard, whom Sharon had been seeing while married to Michael. Frank came from Nova Scotia and lived in an old run-down hotel across the street from the restaurant where Sharon worked. He had no job or possessions, aside from an old green Ford van. Frank took a job at the local cemetery, digging graves and maintaining the grounds. The family moved into a basement suite and within a few months, Frank and Sharon were married. It was a simple justice of the peace wedding conducted at the courthouse, with the wedding reception held in their home. The marriage ceremony was attended by only a handful of close friends. Kyle was four and a half years old.

Kyle's life consisted of being left with friends or with one of Sharon's sisters while both Frank and Sharon worked. His relationship with Frank remained rather insubstantial, as Frank did not invest any time or energy into it. Instead, Frank spent his free time drinking and partying with his friends - alcoholics and drug addicts. Oftentimes, Frank would take Kyle with him to these parties and leave him alone to play outside or alone in a room in the house. Most of the time, Kyle sat in front of a record player, losing himself in the album artwork or liner sheets until he fell asleep. Sharon would pick him up once she finished work.

Kyle's life with Sharon wasn't much better. While Sharon did ensure that Kyle received three meals a day and was dressed warmly when it was cold, she didn't spend any quality time with Kyle.

Sharon and Frank had a child of their own, Jana, born when Kyle was six. His relationship with his adoptive mother and his stepfather did not improve. In fact, it worsened. With Jana's birth, Frank estranged himself even further from Kyle. He doted on his daughter and forced Kyle to call him "Dad," but he did nothing else to be an actual father figure for Kyle. Instead, Frank continued his partying ways, leaving Kyle home alone with these strict instructions: "Do not leave your bedroom. Study - do *not* touch *anything* in the house." Frank would check for evidence of Kyle watching television or eating any of the household food. If he found Kyle guilty of breaking the rules, there were consequences . . .

Kyle did not experience things that most children get to experience. He never had friends sleep over at his house. Friends were not allowed to come over after school to play, and he was never registered to play on a sports team. He was never taught to play a musical instrument or participate in any type of extracurricular activity. Instead, this now eight-year-old boy spent his entire childhood hearing his stepfather try to beat him down with his words: "You're so stupid!" "You're such a crybaby!" "You're just like your faggot dad!" "You pansy!"

Frank was always trying to beat Kyle down. And he did beat Kyle down, with his hands. He would slap Kyle across the face, grab him by his throat, and pick him up off the ground, smashing his head into the kitchen cupboard, all the while yelling at him with spit flying from his mouth, landing on Kyle's face. And if Frank didn't feel satisfied with the job his hands were doing, he turned to the belt. He'd order Kyle to wait in his bedroom with his pants pulled down to his ankles. Kyle would begin crying as soon as he heard Frank get up from the kitchen table. The rattling of the metal chair dragging across the linoleum sent shivers down Kyle's spine. He could hear Frank's footsteps as he walked to his own bedroom, opened his closet, and dragged the rolled-up belt across the shelf. Finally, he'd hear the buckle tap against the leather, and Frank would appear seconds later. The tears then intensified from the humiliation of standing there naked and knowing what was coming next. Frank would sit on the bed and ask Kyle, "Do you want something to really cry about? Bend over." Kyle was ordered to bend over Frank's knees. He could sense the folded belt being raised in the air, and then he could hear the snap of it hit his bare skin. Kyle would bounce off Frank's knee, screaming from the top of his lungs, begging Frank to stop. Frank, though, often grinned and ordered a second lashing . . . and then a third . . . and a fourth . . .

To add to the adversities Kyle faced, Frank didn't tolerate any sibling rivalry between Kyle and Jana. If Frank caught Kyle teasing Jana, the consequences were dire. One day the two children were in the living room, where they were teasing and arguing with one another. Frank burst into the living room, and Kyle immediately bounced up from the floor into a padded couch chair for any protection he could find. Frank leaned over Kyle and began slapping his head back and forth like a basketball. His bloodshot eyes burned through Kyle as his red face began screaming profanities. Between the air being forced into his eardrums from Frank's cupped hands, and the speed of the blows, Kyle could not make out any of the words. All he could hear were the sounds that came from inside his head from the connection of each thrust. The stench of Frank's breath and the constant spray of spit flying from his mouth nauseated Kyle. Kyle could feel vomit make its way up to his mouth, but he knew things would only get worse should he let it out. He forced it back down and waited for the beating to end.

Frank also picked on Kyle during mealtime. They sat straight across from each other at the kitchen table. "Your dad is such a pussy faggot," Frank would taunt. Kyle would stare with eyes of pure hatred, only to have his knuckles smashed with Frank's fork. Kyle's head would drop in defeat, and tears rolled down his cheeks into his food.

Kyle often cried himself to sleep at night. He didn't live in a religious home, but he knew of God. He'd stare up at his ceiling and ask God why this was happening. He hadn't done anything wrong; he just wanted to be a kid.

Most of the abuse happened while Sharon was at work, but not all of it, and only during extreme cases did she ever intervene. Sharon's own fears prevented her from protecting her son. The family was gathered in the living room one evening enjoying a pizza night. Frank had been drinking all day, and he started in on Kyle, who was lying on the floor in his pajamas, watching television. Taunting and teasing Kyle, Frank's temper escalated. He jumped from his chair and landed on top of Kyle, punching and kicking him as hard as he could. Sharon scurried from the couch and pushed her way between the two. Frank threw her down to the ground. Before Kyle could see what else was going to happen to his mother, he ran out the front door. Kyle ran over ten blocks in his bare feet to the safety of an aunt and uncle's home.

A few hours later, Sharon arrived and took both children to a hotel for the night. She assured Kyle that they didn't have to go back to their home. The next morning they had no clothes with them, no personal belongings, no money, and nowhere to go so they found themselves driving back home. Frank was sitting at the kitchen table crying, wearing the same clothes he'd had on the night before. He had obviously never gone to bed and had stayed up the entire night writing Sharon a letter of apology. He begged her not to leave him. He promised it would never happen again. She stayed. Kyle never received an apology.

At times, Sharon also abused Kyle. Bath time was only once a week, Sunday nights. She'd run a clean, warm bath for Jana, and once she was done, Kyle's mother would call him for his bath. Kyle would cry and beg his mother to let him have a fresh bath, but Sharon insisted that there was nothing wrong with using his sister's bathwater. The more Kyle refused to get into the tub, the angrier Sharon became. If he didn't get into the bath, she slapped him and forced to get in anyway.

Whenever Kyle was caught lying to his mother, she made him stick his tongue out as she poured drops of Tabasco sauce onto it. He was then ordered to stand in the corner, with his tongue sticking out, until she felt a lesson had been learned.

Kyle wasn't able to find safety and comfort at school either. Frank and Sharon's money went to support Frank's habits. Kyle didn't go to school with brand-name clothes. He wore secondhand clothes. The new clothes that he did get once a year were generic brands from Kmart or the SAAN store. He wore cheap shoes and had cheap haircuts. The kids at school ridiculed him and bullied him for his inability to fit in. Groups of boys picked fights with him. Kyle could never win those fights. He was shoved in the hallways and called names such as "loser," "faggot," and "poor boy". Being bullied and judged by one's peers is such a degrading, violating, intimidating feeling.

Kyle had one saving grace in his life: his visits with his adoptive dad, Michael. Michael received visitation every other weekend and for two weeks during summer holidays. He'd pick Kyle up at five o'clock on a Friday and return him home around the same time the next evening. Michael never hit Kyle and never made Kyle feel anything less than his son. He took him to the park, played Frisbee with him, and pushed him on the swings. He took him to restaurants and fast-food chains, something that didn't happen very often in Frank's household.

At Christmastime, Kyle would get one or two toys from Frank and Sharon, but he'd watch his sister, Jana, open dozens of gifts. He did get to see Michael and his grandmother Beverly on Boxing Day and that's when it truly felt like Christmas to Kyle. Over the summer holidays, Michael took Kyle camping and to amusement parks. Kyle was able to be a kid when he was with his dad. For twenty-four hours every second week, Kyle could forget about all his worries and just enjoy being.

Kyle cried when he knew that his visit with his dad would soon be over. He'd beg and plead with his father not to take him back there. Michael knew about the abuse but felt helpless. Frank was a large, intimidating man, and Michael was not. One day he had finally had enough of hearing Kyle's stories of abuse, and at the end of their weekend visit, as he dropped Kyle off at home, he got out of his car and confronted Frank. "What the hell are you doing beating up on my son?" Michael asked. Unfortunately, Frank was not the kind of guy to confront. Frank only knew anger and violence. He beat Michael up in front of Kyle. Kyle was devastated to see the man he loved beaten up by the man he hated so very much.

A few months later, Michael decided to fight for custody of Kyle. It wasn't until Michael's lawyer requested that Kyle testify in court that Frank and Sharon finally signed over custody. They didn't want their dirty laundry aired out in public for everyone to see. So at twelve years old, Kyle was finally going to live with his dad.

CHAPTER 2 –
Good Times

Michael

Living with his father was a dream come true for Kyle. No more would he live in fear. He moved in at the beginning of the summer and did all the things that children his age do. He quickly made friends with children from the neighborhood. He spent the summer at the swimming pool, bike riding, and playing at the park. Life was good. Life was so incredibly good.

When Michael and Sharon divorced, Michael had been forced to sell the house. Since that time, he had lived in low-income housing units and apartments. He and Kyle lived in a five-hundred-square-foot shack, a forty-year-old condominium-type home beside the train tracks. Kyle didn't care where they lived, but it was always Michael's dream to own his own house again. In order to make his dream a reality, Michael took on a second job doing custodial work in the evenings at the local detention center. He'd leave for work in the mornings at eight o'clock, come home for a quick lunch, return to work until five thirty, come home for a quick supper, and head to his second job at six thirty, working until eleven o'clock at night. He did this Mondays through Fridays and was sometimes called into work on the weekends. As a result, Kyle was left at home by himself.

In order to help out, Kyle began preparing lunches. Kyle wanted to have lunch with his dad, often soup and a sandwich, before Michael had to return to work. Then Kyle began testing his cooking skills further and prepared suppers so that Michael wouldn't have to rush home and cook dinner before he went to work again. Kyle didn't mind helping his dad. He had even given Michael three hundred dollars he had saved up from birthdays and cutting lawns to help with the down payment of their new house. Touched by the gesture, Michael promised to pay the money back in time.

At the beginning of summer after Kyle's thirteenth birthday, they took possession of their new home. It was an older house, previously owned by an elderly woman who had done a good job taking care of it. Both Michael and Kyle were so happy to be moving into the house. The basement was unfinished, but Michael had dreams of developing it. Each day before he went to work, he left Kyle with instructions on chores for the day. Kyle's summer filled up with landscaping, painting and small renovation projects. Suddenly, Kyle had little time to spend with friends. Michael believed that since he had to work two jobs to support the family, Kyle needed to work as well. Kyle was expected to prepare all the meals, do the dishes, clean the house, do the laundry, cut the grass in the summer, and shovel the snow in the winter. The responsibilities of the entire household fell on this thirteen-year-old boy's shoulders.

As the months passed, Michael grew tired and worn out from working two jobs. He became frustrated and agitated over trivial matters. He had gone from being a part-time father to a full-time single dad of a thirteen-year-old boy. It was becoming apparent that he simply did not have the skills to do so. His parenting became authoritative and controlling. He demanded to know how Kyle planned to spend his free time. If Michael thought that his plans weren't productive, he would assign more chores. When Michael came home from work, he inspected the work that was completed and was critical about how it was done. Michael was a perfectionist who did not accept anything less from others.

Kyle began to fear his father. He became anxious when he knew his father was coming home. Michael's frustrations in life grew and grew . . . until the day it finally happened. During a routine argument, Michael slapped Kyle across the face. Kyle's eyes immediately welled up with tears. The stinging pain did not bring on the tears; instead, it was the incredible disappointment that he felt toward his father. Michael began crying himself. The guilt had hit him as hard as his slap. He immediately began apologizing and assured Kyle that it would never happen again. For the first time in almost a year, Kyle saw a glimmer of the father that he used to have before they ever bought the house - the father he had loved and adored. This glimmer of the father Michael had been when he first received custody of Kyle helped him to forgive Michael. The two of them spent the day together in peace.

It didn't take long, though, for the high levels of stress and frustration to return to both their lives. Michael began calling Kyle names like "bastard" and saying things like, "you don't have a god damn brain." Michael blamed Kyle for his problems. To some extent, Michael felt that Kyle had ruined his life. Through the custody battle and in raising him, Michael felt that Kyle had cost him too much money. Most of their fights were with words, but as the months went on, Michael continued to grow angrier about his life. Then the beatings were suddenly happening all the time. Michael slapped or punched Kyle during any disagreements or arguments that arose, never showing remorse.

Kyle loved reading comic books – the magical worlds full of super heroes who always conquered over the presence of evil. It was his escape from reality. While Kyle was lying on his bedroom floor reading a comic book, Michael one day burst into the room, kicked him in the stomach as hard as he could, and left. Kyle vomited on the floor from the impact and the pain. He had no idea what he had done.

Abuse is like so many things in life. If left unattended, it can grow into an even bigger and even uglier monster. Kyle was now fourteen. Life had been rather consistent over the last year. Tiptoeing around his father, completely following through on all instructions and knowing that when he didn't, he'd have to deal with the consequences, Kyle lived in fear. Once again, Kyle lived with abuse.

Kyle was preparing supper one evening, as he had done hundreds of times before. Michael had come home in an even more pissed-off mood than usual. He criticized the meal that Kyle prepared and stated that he wouldn't eat this garbage. He threw the food in the trash and made himself some toast. The two of them sat down at the kitchen table together.

"I thought I told you to tell your girlfriends not to call after midnight," Michael scorned.

"I did tell them. I'm sorry. I don't know why she called so late last night," Kyle responded.

Michael's voice began to get louder as he yelled, "You know I have to get up early in the morning! I won't tolerate this in my house!"

"Yeah, I get it! It won't happen again. You don't have to fricken yell at me," Kyle screamed back.

Kyle turned his attention down toward his plate to avoid his father's burning stare. Suddenly, Kyle's body became flushed with an incredible amount of heat and pain. His head immediately began to throb, and his ear began ringing, muffling all sounds. Michael had reached across the table and punched Kyle in the ear. Kyle had fallen out of his chair and onto the floor. He positioned himself on all fours as a means of trying to stand up. He couldn't though, because Michael was standing in front and over top of him. He punched Kyle repeatedly on the ears, kneed his ribs, and pulled his hair.

At fourteen, Kyle was tired of letting people abuse him. His whole life it was either Frank, the kids at school, or his father, Michael. For the first time in his life, Kyle decided to fight back. He channeled all his energy and exploded. The force of this internal combustion brought Kyle to his feet. As he began to stand, he pushed Michael in the chest, using both his hands and all his strength. Michael was caught off guard and sent flying back into a door-jamb. As his body smashed into the corner of the door-jamb, Michael immediately slithered to the floor in defeat.

For the first time in Kyle's life, he felt strong and empowered. Tears poured from his eyes as he screamed, "Fuck you, you piece of shit! *Fuck you!*"

Michael looked up at Kyle. With his last bit of energy, he yelled, "No, fuck you! Get the fuck out of my house! I never want to see you again!"

At one time, Kyle had looked at his father as a man who could do no wrong. That day, he had broken Kyle's heart.

CHAPTER 3 –
A New Life

George, Dana, and Kerry

Kyle was just a kid, a kid in foster care. After an investigation by police and social workers, it was determined that Kyle couldn't return to his father's care, nor did he want to. The previous year, Kyle had developed a friendship with another boy at school. His name was Kerry. The two boys grew to be inseparable best friends, almost like brothers. When things used to get bad at home, Kyle would take shelter at Kerry's. Kerry's parents liked Kyle. He was always welcomed there for dinners or sleepovers. The night that Kyle was kicked out of his house, he found himself at Kerry's. Kerry's parents wanted to help Kyle and offered to let him stay as long as he needed to. They even applied to become foster parents. Social Services agreed that this would be a good home for Kyle and granted their application.

Kerry's father, George, was a good, honest, hardworking family man who enjoyed teaching the boys mechanical repair and taking them fishing. Dana, Kerry's mother, was a nurturing, kind woman who kept an immaculate home and prepared amazing family dinners.

Kyle enjoyed being part of their family. He and Kerry hung around together at school, after school, and even got their first part-time jobs together as dishwashers at the same restaurant. The boys enjoyed hard and fast music and had an unlimited supply of black T-shirts with band logos on them. They even liked to act a little wild every once in awhile. They were fifteen years old and trying to figure out how they fit into this crazy world.

Sometimes on weekends, they liked to share a few beers together, but what they liked most was the taste of whiskey and the buzz they got from a night of drinking it. They would often plan weekend fishing trips and take a bottle of whiskey with them. Kyle also enjoyed a cigarette and a joint on occasion. Kerry didn't smoke cigarettes, and he definitely didn't want to have anything to do with drugs. Kyle always respected his friend's decision to stay away from drugs, but Kyle loved the freedom and ability to escape reality, which getting high brought him.

Kyle soon found himself hanging out with some of the older kids at school, the ones who liked to party and get high. He tried to include Kerry in his new group of friends, but Kerry wasn't interested. Kyle, however, loved hanging out with these new guys. They were just like him. They all came from shitty homes where they were abused by their parents, kicked out, or unwanted. They all had a "Fuck you, world" attitude, and they found safety, strength, and comfort in each other.

Kyle partied nearly every weekend, sometimes not coming home for days. His drug use intensified, and his relationship with Kerry slowly deteriorated until the boys no longer had anything in common. Kerry's parents decided that they did not sign up for this type of behavior or this type of child, and they told Kyle that they wanted him out of their house. His foster care placement with them had only lasted five months. And again, he had nowhere to go.

When Kyle was fourteen, and still living with Michael, he was forced to see a family therapist. At that time, when things were chaotic in the household, Michael believed Kyle's anger and attitude were the problem. Michael ordered Kyle to see the therapist and said that he would attend as well. Kyle refused to comply and thought that there was no way he was going to let some "head-shrink" mess with his mind. After several arguments, Kyle reluctantly agreed.

The family therapist that Kyle met with was named Lee. She was a gentle soul, and Kyle immediately liked her. He found comfort talking to her and sometimes felt that she was the only person who ever understood him. Michael and Kyle went to two separate sessions with her. Kyle enjoyed having this new outlet to share his feelings, but Michael didn't like what the therapist had to say and never went back. Kyle continued to see her once a week for a year. He had an appointment with her the week that he was kicked out of Kerry's house. As he sat in the waiting room, he saw a familiar face; it was Lynne, a social worker who was also Kyle and Michael's next-door neighbor during the time Kyle lived with Michael.

Lynne and Rick

Lynne's was a comforting face to see. She asked Kyle what he was doing there. He explained his current situation of not having anywhere to live. She invited him to come over to her place that night so they could talk. Lynne lived with her common-law partner, Rick, an outdoors kind of man who loved hunting and fishing. She had a son who was four years younger than Kyle. While they were neighbors, she often asked Kyle to come over and babysit for her. They had Kyle do odd jobs around the yard for them. Rick would poke his head over the fence when he came home from work. If he saw Kyle in the yard working, he'd strike up conversation and always make a few jokes. Kyle liked this couple and got excited when Rick invited him on fishing trips. After Michael bought his house, he had stopped doing father and son things with Kyle. In many ways, Rick was that father figure that Kyle so desperately wanted.

After school, Kyle quickly made his way to Lynne's house. Fortunately, she no longer lived next door to Michael. Kyle was so excited to see her and knew that somehow she could help him out. After all, she had always been there when things got bad with Michael. Kyle once again explained his predicament about not having anywhere to live and how his life just seemed to continue to fall apart. Lynne suggested that he stay with her and Rick. Kyle's eyes lit up, as he could not believe her gesture of kindness. Could it be for real?

Social workers are not supposed to get emotionally involved with their clients, and even though Kyle was not one of her assigned cases, it was considered taboo for her to become a foster parent to him. Social Services strongly suggested that she not follow through. They even refused her financial support. Lynne was persistent, and she and Rick soon became Kyle's second foster parents.

Kyle absolutely loved living with that family. He truly felt part of it and asked Lynne one day if he could call her "Mom." He felt awesome. He had a mother, a father and even a little brother. The two boys got into petty arguments at times. Kyle would sometimes find himself picking on John, but the sibling rivalry made it all that much more real to Kyle. He loved it!

That first Christmas was Kyle's favorite Christmas of all time. That morning, he and John ran down the stairs to a beautiful Christmas tree and an ocean of presents. He was fifteen years old, but he felt as if he were eight again. The wondrous smells coming from the kitchen and the laughter in the house of friends and family who came over to visit filled Kyle's heart with peace. Every now and then, he would experience his body feeling flushed with a sense of peace and contentment from living there. His eyes would begin to well up. In his mind, he would thank God.

For the first few months of living with Lynne and Rick, they let Kyle continue living his life the way he had been. He continued to stay out late and party with his friends, and he continued drinking. After a few months of this, Lynne sat Kyle down one night. She explained that if he continued staying out late, partying with his friends, he would have to leave. If he began making changes, he could stay. It wasn't a hard decision for Kyle. His whole life, all he'd wanted was to be part of a family. He didn't make the changes overnight, but he began to withdraw from his group of friends. He stopped staying out all night, cutting drugs and alcohol out of his life.

Kyle's life was good. Before a year of living with this family had passed, Lynne sat Kyle down for another talk. She told him that the family had decided that they were moving to another province. She said that they wouldn't be taking Kyle with them. When Kyle asked why he couldn't go with them, Lynne offered no explanation other than he wasn't their responsibility.

Frustrated, angry, and sad, Kyle began having suicidal thoughts and the family had not quite moved yet. One day, while Rick and Lynne were at work, Kyle skipped school, stayed home, and made his way down to the unfinished basement. It was cold. Goosebumps ran up his arm and down his neck as he thought, *"If I kill myself, everyone in my entire life will feel bad for the way they treated me. If I kill myself, they will all finally realize what a great guy I was."* As tears trickled down his face, Kyle made a noose out of an extension cord. He climbed up onto a table and tied it to the ceiling rafters. He put the noose around his neck and swayed back and forth on the edge of the table. He only wished that he could somehow see the look on their faces when they came home to find him. He continued to sway back and forth all afternoon, the trickling tears now pouring down his face. Hours passed, and the noose tightened as Kyle leaned farther over the table.

Maybe it was the fear of dying or maybe it was the hope of living that prevented Kyle from hanging himself. As the last few tears rolled off his cheeks and onto the floor, he made a decision. Kyle promised himself that he would never allow himself to get close to anyone ever again. Every time he got close to someone, he was left hurt, disappointed, or worse. He knew that if he never allowed himself to get close to anyone ever again, he would never have to feel this pain again. As those last few tears rolled off his cheeks, he knew they would be the last tears he'd ever shed for anyone, ever.

CHAPTER 4 - Independence

When Lynne and Rick moved away, Kyle went into the Single Independent Living Program, a government-subsidized program for teenagers. The program pays a teenager's rent, provides food and clothing allowances, and pays for school tuition and books. It is often a program of last resort. When foster care fails, when there is no family to live with, and when a young person is at least sixteen years of age, they may qualify for the program. Kyle was now sixteen and had found himself a basement suite which he rented in the home of a German couple who were the parents of one of his new friends, Kevin. He and Kevin shared the basement suite together.

No parents, no rules, and no one to disappoint him or let him down . . . For some youths, this sounds like a perfect life. For Kyle, this independence became very self-destructive. Kyle began drinking every weekend, partying with his friends. During the week, he often drank by himself. The more drunk he got, the better he felt. He and his friends often found some house party to attend. If there wasn't one, they'd take their booze down into the coulees and make their own party. Many nights, Kyle would stumble home, swaying back and forth and talking aloud to himself. His conversations were a means of trying to figure out what exactly had happened in his life that brought him to where he was now.

School was definitely not a priority. He began failing most of his classes. His previous grades ranging from 79 to 81 percent dropped to between 42 and 51 percent. He'd fall asleep during class. He rarely turned in a homework assignment, and he would randomly fill in the circles of any multiple choice exams. His truancy numbers were the highest his guidance counselor had ever seen. Instead of attending classes, Kyle slept his days away. When he did go to school, he was the class clown. He learned at a young age that to get positive attention, all he had to do was make people laugh. During the teacher's lectures, he crawled around the classroom tying the other students shoelaces to the legs of their desk. He even stuffed toilet paper into their shoes while they were wearing them. The best pranks were the ones he pulled on the teachers. Those won his peers over the most. Of course, the pranks didn't go over well with the teachers. As an example, in health class, when he found out the teacher would be showing a video on drug addiction, Kyle swapped the video tape with a Cheech & Chong movie. He set the tape to the part where Chong smashes a cockroach on the table, stuffs it in a pipe, and tries to smoke it.

Kyle's school guidance counselor, Mr. McFarlane, had a soft spot for the troubled teenager. He tried to do as much as he could to keep Kyle from getting kicked out of school. He helped Kyle find a part-time job and always welcomed Kyle into his office. As much as Mr. McFarlane wanted to see Kyle succeed, he assured Kyle that there was no way that he would graduate high school.

Kyle was an active drug user. He had tried drugs for the first time when he was eleven years old. Back in the days when Frank was partying every weekend, on the occasions when he did bring Kyle along, Kyle sometimes hung around the children of Frank's friends. There was always an abundance of drugs around. Some of Frank's friends even had hydroponic grow operations in their basements for marijuana. Kyle and his weekend friends stole cigarettes and marijuana at these parties and headed off to the park to smoke. Smoking drugs like marijuana followed Kyle throughout his life as a teenager. By the time he was sixteen, smoking pot had grown from occasional use to as often as he could. Smoking pot was great, but getting his hands on some oil or hashish was even better. As time went on, Kyle's frequency of drug use increased. The types of drugs he was using grew in selection.

When you're on a path of self-destruction - when you are angry, frustrated, and alone - crime can be something you easily fall into . . . or rather an easy choice to make. Like so many of the other things mentioned in this book, it can start off relatively small and simple, but it can grow into something big and out of control. Have you ever started something small . . . only to watch it grow and grow?

Kyle and his friends loved cruising around in their cars. More often than not, no one had any gas money. Kyle found a solution to the problem. Kyle's next-door neighbor always left his garden hose strung out on his lawn after watering. Late at night, the group of boys would take a pair of hedge clippers and cut a length of hose right from

> Have you ever started something small . . . only to watch it grow and grow?

23

the middle of the hose. They'd grab their gas cans and sneak through the back alleys until they found a vehicle with an unlocked gas cap. They would then proceed to siphon the gas until their gas cans were full. After each gas theft, they threw away the length of hose to dispose of the evidence. When they needed gas again, they'd repeat the exact same procedure including cutting the length of hose from the neighbor. Kyle's next-door neighbor, who happened to be a police officer, often asked Kyle if he ever saw anyone cutting his garden hose. Of course, Kyle's response was always 'No'.

As Kyle and his friends cruised around town, they'd eventually get hungry and require the other kind of fuel: food. Five or six of the boys would head into the late night convenience store. They'd make their way to strategic locations throughout the store. They would take turns distracting the clerk by asking how much a certain item cost, holding the item up in the air. Meanwhile, the other guys stuffed their jackets full of chocolate bars, chips, and cigarettes. As they left the store, a couple of boys bought one small item so as not to raise suspicion for their next visit.

When full darkness had set in and most city residents were fast asleep, Kyle and his friends walked up and down the streets of the neighborhood and checked the door handle of each vehicle. If a door happened to be unlocked, the boys quietly entered, and looted through the entire vehicle. They stole spare change, CDs, and sometimes even a few treasures.

Small juvenile crimes such as these simply became a part of Kyle's life, until the night Kyle and two of his friends robbed a gas station.

CHAPTER 5 –
Who Will Cry for the Little Boy

This little boy experienced so much pain and disappointment in his life, but all he ever wanted was to be a little boy, to play, to laugh, to be loved, to feel safe, to be free and to be part of a family. Time wasn't on his side, though, and before he knew it, he was a man.

I tell Kyle's story at conferences and events all across North America. I ask the audience what they think happened to Kyle - where they thought those paths of self-destruction led. I get responses such as him ending up in jail, dying of a drug overdose, growing up to be an alcoholic, or killing himself. All of these are possible and probable when we look at the different stages of Kyle's life. People know that the path Kyle was on could not end anywhere good. Where did his path lead?

One of my favorite movies is *Antwone Fisher* which features and was directed by Denzel Washington. If you connected with Kyle's story, I venture to guess that you would enjoy this movie as well. It is a true story of the life of Antwone Fischer and the incredible adversity he faced as a child. Antwone wrote a poem that I always thought was a perfect fit for Kyle's story.

Who Will Cry for the Little Boy?
By Antwone Fischer

Who will cry for the little boy, lost and all alone?

Who will cry for the little boy, abandoned without his own?

Who will cry for the little boy? He cried himself to sleep.

Who will cry for the little boy? He never had for keeps.

Who will cry for the little boy? He walked the burning sand.

Who will cry for the little boy? The boy inside the man.

Who will cry for the little boy? He knows well hurt and pain.

Who will cry for the little boy? He died and died again.

Who will cry for the little boy? A good boy he tried to be.

Who will cry for the little boy, who cries inside of me?

So what happened to Kyle?

However improbable it may be to believe, Kyle pulled it off and actually graduated from high school, and he even went on to attend and graduate from college. He became a volunteer in his community and dedicated his life to working with young people. He wanted to make a difference for those who experience pains similar to the ones he had experienced. He wanted to create "ripples." Most recently, Kyle began writing chapter 5 of the book you are now reading.

Kyle's story is my story. One of the first things I tell audiences, once they realize that Kyle is in fact me, is that my story is no more significant or important than that of anyone in the room or, in this case, anyone reading this book. Absolutely every person in the world has a story to tell – his or her story . . . your story. Everyone who has a past has a story.

I do not share Kyle's story, my story, to gain sympathy. Human beings are drawn to the tragedy of an event. Just check the Internet and see what the top stories featured on all the major news sites are about. We love hearing about the drama and tragedy in the world. However, if we spend most of our energy focusing on the tragedy of an event or story, we often miss out on the lesson or opportunity. The significance of this story is not in the sadness and pain, but rather rejoicing in the hope and ability to overcome adversity. Kyle's story has a happy ending, or rather a happy new beginning, and I'll tell you more about Kyle's story in the upcoming chapters.

Adversity is an amazing monster that excludes no one. It doesn't matter whether you are the richest kid in your community or the poorest; adversity excludes no one. We can't escape it either. No matter what level of success, status, wealth, or love you achieve in your life, you will continue to be faced with adversity. This sounds terrible and worse than it needs to be. Yes, we all experience adversity and trauma in our lives. Yes, we will continue to be confronted with old and new adversities and traumas, but there is hope.

In order for us to learn how to overcome adversity, we must ask ourselves a few important questions: Why do some people who endure incredible amounts of adversity in their lives grow up to be contributing members of their communities, able to create and maintain "normal" healthy relationships and go on to lead healthy and harmonious lives? Yet why do other people who endure the same levels of adversity, or even less, go on to repeat the cycles of abuse and/or addictions into adulthood, never able to break free of the pain and sadness in their lives, therefore continuing to create more pain and sadness?

The answer to these questions is one simple word: resiliency. Resiliency is a universal capacity that allows a person, group, or community to prevent, minimize, or overcome the damaging effects of adversity.

As a society, we must understand and appreciate the power of resiliency if we want to create more happy endings and happy beginnings. Whether you are a child, teacher, social worker, parent, guardian or survivor of adversity, it is important to know that we must apply the concepts of resiliency in order to break the cycles that are preventing our youths, our students, and even ourselves from obtaining healthy, harmonious lives. Our society continues to be on the reactive side when it comes to the economy or people's health and wellness. We spend little effort finding proactive solutions. We have thousands of centers for addictions, detention centers, rehab facilities, and shelters as our response to the damaging effects of adversity. It is only since the late 1990s that we have begun putting energy into proactive programs and initiatives in our schools and communities, but so much more needs to be done. Understanding, promoting, and applying the concepts of resilience is important because "it is the human capacity to face, overcome and be strengthened by or even transformed by the adversities of life" (Grotberg, 1995). With resiliency, children can triumph over trauma; without it, trauma (adversity) triumphs. The crises children face both within their families and in their communities can overwhelm them.

For the Bernard van Leer Foundation, Dr. Edith H. Grotberg produced the publication "A Guide to Promoting Resilience in Children: Strengthening the Human Spirit." Dr. Grotberg was the first to introduce the theory of resiliency to the helping professions. She dedicated her life's work to the well-being of others.

Dr. Grotberg created the I HAVE, I AM, I CAN model in order to explain the three groups of factors that promote resilience:

I HAVE – These are supports, resources, and help outside of the child. They are external supports and resources that can be provided by the family, other significant people, and the community. If a child possesses this feature, she believes and/or knows that she has people around her whom she trusts and whom love her no matter what. The child has people whom set limits for her, so she knows when to stop before there is danger or trouble. Children who have the I HAVE model have role models in their lives who show them how to do things. These role models also allow the children to learn to do things on their own. These supports are people who help the children when they are sick or in danger.

If a child has people she can trust, love or like, and respect, then the child has I HAVE people. Such people will teach the child how to be safe by putting structures with limits around her. I HAVE people show children how to behave; they model good behavior; they encourage children to be able to do things for themselves - to be independent; and they explain the facilities and services available for use.

I AM – These are internal feelings, attitudes, beliefs, and strengths developed within the child. These stay with the child throughout his life. They can be strengthened but cannot be created. A child who possesses I AM believes he is a person whom people can like and love. The child is glad to do nice things for others and demonstrate his concern. The I AM child is respectful of others and himself. He is responsible for what he does; he has optimism and trust; and he is confident things will turn out all right.

I CAN – These are social, interpersonal, and problem-solving skills that children learn and acquire. These are tools for interacting with other people. They must be taught and learned. It is the ability to say, "I can talk to others about things that frighten or bother me. I can find ways to solve problems that I face. I can control myself when I feel like doing something not right or dangerous." These children can find someone to help them when they need it, and they can figure out when is a good time to talk to someone or take action. They can think of new or creative ways of doing things and can stay with a task until it is completed.

According to the International Resiliency Project, a child does not have to have all these features, but one is not enough. A child may be loved (I HAVE), but if the child has no inner strength (I AM) or social, interpersonal skills (I CAN), there can be no resilience. To be resilient, a child must possess at least two of the three features in order to triumph adversity.

Adversity comes in many shapes and sizes. In Kyle's story, we looked at adoption, divorce, remarriage, mental abuse, physical abuse, abandonment, and various other adversities. Adversity can also reveal itself in the faces of things like poverty, poor health and hospitalization, death or illness of a parent or sibling, war, robberies, moving away from family and friends ... and the list can go on and on and on. What we are finding is that when there are too many adverse factors, children's abilities to perform cognitive tasks are adversely affected, and their IQs drop.

In my own journey of gaining knowledge and understanding of resiliency, I was able to realize that Kyle had unknowingly utilized these three resilient factors in his journey of overcoming adversity. In my own healing and searching, I have identified five tools that you can use to become more resilient and triumph over adversity. These tools are outlined in the following chapters.

Chapter 6 –
Breaking the Cycles

Tool number one is breaking the cycles. It starts with choice. We can choose a different path. Right where we left off in Kyle's story, I had come to a true crossroads in my life. I could continue down the path that I was on, the path of anger, alcohol, drugs, and crime, and likely repeat the cycles of abuse and addictions I had grown up with, or I could travel an unfamiliar path. I could start a new path where I would need to be accountable for my own life – a path where I would take control over that life.

You see, abuse and addictions are cycles that are passed down from generation to generation. Society, as a whole, does this on even grander scales. All we have to do is take a history lesson and look at the adverse effects of war and the diminishing impact we are having on our natural environment. For centuries, we have continued to kill one another out of acts of power, religion, politics, and hatred. Our lack of compassion and our inability to learn from our mistakes has caused us to continue to repeat these acts of violence against one another. This is leaving our planet in disarray. Should we allow history to continue to repeat itself, it may very well result in our own demise.

Taking it back to the micro scale, behaviors such as addictions and abuse will continue repeating themselves if our generation does not consciously put a stop to them now. It is believed by practitioners that the majority of family abuse is unreported, which makes it difficult to create accurate statistics. However, many practitioners believe that if you grew up in a home where you were sexually, emotionally, or physically abused, you have an 80 percent chance of abusing your own children or partner. If you grew up in a home of alcoholism or drug addiction, you have an 80 percent chance of becoming a drug addict or alcoholic yourself. An 80 percent chance! In other words, statistics tell us that you are more than likely to repeat the same behaviors that caused *you* so much pain as a child. The problem is that you are going to continue to create more pain in your life and, possibly worse, create pain in the lives of others as well.

Think of it as a loop. At the top of the loop, you find people like Frank's parents. They abuse him as a child. We move along the loop, and Frank abuses me as a child. As we continue to move around this loop, what is the next logical step? The answer, of course, is that I end up abusing my own children. The good news is that I have the power to stop the flow of this loop. I have the ability to stop history from repeating itself. I simply have to choose to break the cycles.

When I turned eighteen and graduated from high school, I decided that I needed to move away from where I had grown up. I wanted to start over. I wanted to be somewhere where no one knew me. I accepted a job as a painter in North Battleford, Saskatchewan.

I lived there for about a year and rarely returned to my hometown even for quick visits. When I did, I always visited my grandmother Beverley. She was Michael's mother, and she had always treated me with love and kindness, no matter what trouble I was getting into. During one of these visits, she had handed me a newspaper article that she had cut out. The heading of the article was WOMAN'S TESTIMONY CONVICTS MAN OF SEXUAL ASSUALT. From reading the article, I learned that Frank had been convicted of raping the woman. I knew I didn't want to be just like him. My first response to the article was that of pure joy. Finally, Frank had gotten what was coming to him. After all the years of being a jerk, justice had been served. My feeling of satisfaction was short-lived though, as my attention drifted from Frank to the poor woman in the article. My heart went out to her. Then, as I read the article again, my mind became stuck on the mention of Sharon. She had been quoted that she felt he was innocent.

Completely unaware of where I was headed, I found myself driving to Frank and Sharon's house. It had been over seven years since I had last been there, and amazingly enough, in those seven years I had not even bumped into them in the community. The house had not changed a bit, and my stomach began tying itself into knots as I walked up the driveway. I knocked on the door and Sharon answered. Tears immediately poured from her eyes. I explained to her that my intention was not to rejoin her family but to help her in whatever way I could. I told her that I would help her find a new home and help her move. I tried to fill her in on what I had done during my seven years away, but I really wasn't there to prove to her that I had managed fine without her. She minimized and dismissed parts of my past, and I began feeling angry and resentful toward her; I would have settled for an apology. I thought that with society reinforcing the truth of Frank's violent behavior by locking him up, she might finally see the man he really was. Sharon did not believe that Frank was capable of such an act and went on to explain that she planned to wait for him until he was released. Sharon looked me in the eyes and said that all the abuse I endured was in my head, and that the times I did get hit, I deserved it. I tried to convince her otherwise but was unsuccessful. I wasn't sure if she believed his innocence or if she was afraid of what he would do to her if she did not stand by him.

I continued to visit Sharon over the next couple of years, coming by the house every month or two. I thought that she'd come around in time. I repeatedly explained to her that when Frank was released from prison, I would no longer have a relationship with her if she went back to him. She fully understood, and we continued to have our visits together. When Christmas-time came, I was feeling terrible that she and Jana would be spending it alone. I had picked up a card for them and called to ask if they wanted some company. She invited me over. When I arrived, a few of Frank's relatives were visiting. I felt obligated to come in for a few minutes, and I proceeded to the kitchen. To my surprise, Frank was sitting at the kitchen table. All the anger and fear I had experienced as a child flowed through my veins like hot lava. I felt betrayed again. How could she welcome him into her home after all the displays of kindness and support I had shown her while he was in jail? How could she trust and believe him when she never trusted or believed her own child? How could she invite me over when she knew of my hatred for this man? I was in shock. Frank asked me a few questions, but I didn't respond, and after three obligatory sips of coffee, I escaped. I never went back, and I have not seen Sharon since. However, I have learned Sharon's motivation. People make decisions based on past experience and available resources. Sharon's upbringing was not a lot better than mine, and her supports and resources were minimal. Frank, it seemed, took advantage of those deficits.

I couldn't allow myself to be like Frank or Sharon. As the cycles of abuse and addictions continued their way around the loop, I made a firm commitment to myself that they stopped here. They stopped with me.

Having the desire, strength and ability to choose to break the cycles addresses our "I AM" and our "I CAN". I am a person that people can like and love. I am a person who is respectful of others and myself. I can find healthy ways to solve problems that I face. I can control myself when I feel like doing something that is wrong or dangerous.

Only we can be the peace our hearts have desired for so long. And to obtain it, we first have to choose it.

CHAPTER 7 –
Identify and Connect with Supports

When I first realized that I had overcome adversity, I was so proud of myself. I thought that I had beaten the odds. As a child, I had felt so alone. So when I triumphed over adversity, I thought I had done it all on my own, without the help of anyone. I could hold my head up high and say to myself, "I did it!"

Right around the time I decided to get into the helping profession and become a youth counselor, I did a lot of reflecting on my life. When I began to take a closer look at my past, I began to realize that I was never alone. Throughout my journey, people had come in and out of my life, helping me along the way. Some of these people were only in my life for a short time, and then they were gone. Others came into my life for a while, then left and reappeared later. And some were there all along, even if I didn't realize it at the time. I'm sure each of you reading this book can identify people in your own life that fit each of these categories.

When it comes right down to it, we simply cannot do it all on our own, regardless of how strong our wills are, how determined we are, or how stubborn we may be. We need the help of others throughout our journeys. We need to identify those people in our lives to whom we can talk with, to whom we connect and trust. In my own life, I had identified teachers, guidance counselors, my friends and their parents, and even a few aunts and uncles who made a significant impact in my life.

As a child and a teenager, I was very ashamed of my story. I carried shame and embarrassment and for the most part, kept my story a secret from all others. I didn't want people to know my humiliation, my fears, or my pain. My relationships had taught me not to trust. Still, every now and then someone would come into my life with whom I felt a connection, and I would slowly let my guard down.

In the eighth grade, I lived in the river valley and had a ten-block walk, up-hill, to get to school. Yes, I know that every child's parents had to walk up-hill ten blocks to get to school, but in my case, it was not an exaggeration. It was the truth. Each morning I ran down to the end of my block, to where I could see the long set of stairs coming down the hill above me, with hopes of seeing my physical education teacher, Mr. Kraft. I was a terribly skinny student with almost no athletic ability, but Mr. Kraft never made me feel bad about that. He always encouraged me and had such a positive outlook on life. I loved the days when I saw him walking down the stairs from the hill because then I got to walk to school with him. I didn't ever share my entire story with him, but I did share parts of it with him ... or even just what had been happening in my life that week. Just his listening and his presence made me feel as if things were going to be all right.

My eleventh grade English teacher, Mrs. Holmes, was one of the few teachers who didn't mind my sense of humor or my class clown antics. In fact, she encouraged it. She'd laugh at my stories, and she was the reason I began to love to write. She nurtured my creativity, and she is one of the reasons this book has come to fruition. She wasn't a teacher with whom I had shared my story. She was simply someone who made me feel good about myself and helped me see that I had potential and could accomplish anything I set my mind to.

The guidance counselor who insisted I would never graduate from high school also tried so hard to help me. Mr. McFarlane signed the government documentation that I needed in order to stay in the Single Independent Living Program. Had my truancies or failing grades been detected, I ran the risk of getting kicked out of the program. I did share most of my story with him, which I am sure is why he did as much as he did. He felt sorry for me, but more importantly, he could see my potential even then. It is thanks to him that I did graduate high school. He made arrangements with my teachers to let me catch up on past-due assignments, and he made me sign a contract that I would not miss one more class in the sixty or so days left in the school year. He made it clear that if I missed even one class, I would get kicked out of school. I'm not sure why, but graduating was something I had to do for myself - and to show everyone else from my past that I was smart enough and capable enough to do it without them.

Years later, dressed in a suit, I was delivering a presentation to a Lions Club in search of sponsorship for a youth initiative on which I was working, and Mr. McFarlane happened to be one of the people in the audience. He couldn't believe his own eyes. He stood up after the presentation and made a public announcement on how far I had come along, and how his group definitely needed to support my youth initiative. It felt good to have him see me up there, not because I was caught up in my own ego or achievements, but because he was one of the people who had been there for me when things were at their worst. Sometimes being a teacher, counselor, or a social worker can seem like a thankless job. We don't get to see immediate results from our efforts. But let me assure you that those of you who are genuine in your approach are making a remarkable difference in the lives of the young people with whom you connect. It goes back to "A Ripple's Reach," - you made a difference to that one; you have made a difference to me. Thank you.

Some of you may be in an existing situation where you are being abused emotionally, sexually, or physically. The first thing to understand is that it is never okay for someone to hit you or touch you in inappropriate ways, absolutely never. It is often our fear of being abused more that prevents us from reaching out. Some often believe that "if they confront my abuser about the abuse, he's only going to get me worse when they are gone."

Abusers often threaten their victims with acts of even more abuse or threaten to hurt someone else they love, or in some cases, even threaten to kill them if they ever disclose the abuse to anyone. It is this fear that our abusers instill in us that prevents us from seeking help. If this sounds like you, then I hope you can understand that there are people out there, such as social workers, child and youth care workers, child protection workers, and police officers, whose number one priority is to protect children. They are people who can help. They are people who want to help. As a child, I never breathed a word to anyone about Frank abusing me. I was so incredibly afraid of him that I kept everything to myself. I knew that if I made him angry, I would get it that much worse. My fear of him kept me his prisoner for over seven years of my life. If I had known then what I know now, I would have done things differently. As cliché as that sounds, it is true. If I had understood that there were people who could have protected me, I would have reached out to them. I hope you find the courage to reach out to them. If you need help right now, I encourage you to go to the "Inspiration" section of my website www.wellnessrealization.net where you will find up-to-date contact information for resources that can and will help you.

Maybe the act of being abused is behind you, but the pain, fear, and memories are not. The horrors of our abuse and adversities can live on in our hearts and minds for years, well beyond when the events actually took place. Even when we think we have escaped it, our minds re-create it repeatedly for us. It follows us into our dreams and thoughts. It keeps us from ever moving on in our lives. Some people carry it with them for a lifetime. When the pain is so heavy that all you want to do is escape it, when the pain is impacting your relationships with other people or your job or your ability to perform at school, maybe it is time to talk to a professional. Psychiatrists, psychologists, family therapists, social workers, and child and youth care workers are there for us when our troubles are too large for us to process ourselves. In most cases, this is a free service as mental health therapy is a subsidized service provided by the government in Canada.

Sometimes our pride prevents us from seeking such help. We think we are strong enough to deal with our own issues, and we definitely aren't crazy. We fear that only crazy people get counseling. Sometimes we are so ashamed or embarrassed by our own stories that we just can't bear sharing them with someone else. These were my excuses. I had a false belief that some 'head-shrink' was going to label me, diagnose me, and play with my mind. I was ashamed of my story and just didn't believe that I needed anyone's help. I believed I could do it on my own. I was wrong.

Fortunately for me, I began to let go of some of those beliefs, and at the age of fourteen, I began to see a family therapist. Looking back, I am so thankful for my time with Lee. Sometimes she would just sit there and listen to me vent my frustrations. She helped me process everything that had happened in my life. Maybe the most significant thing she ever did for me was help me realize that none of the abuse I endured was my fault. Now, as a youth counselor, I can truly appreciate the role that people in the helping professions play in the healing process of others.

People need people.

Our whole life will be created by our experiences and relationships with other people. Not all those experiences will be positive ones. For those experiences that haunt us and impact us in negative ways, people like social workers and child and youth care counselors can help us overcome our adversities.

In situations where our adversities are coming directly from our mothers, fathers, or step-parents, we may be able to find comfort or safety with extended family members. Maybe you have an aunt, uncle, or grandparent with whom you feel a connection to. I had a few aunts and uncles who took an interest in my life. They could sense that things were not quite right in my life, but because I was too uncertain of the outcome, I chose not to share too much of my story with them. Still, I was able to enjoy the times when I saw them, and their presence gave me hope for a better life. Some of them had nice homes, nice things and new cars. I'd watch them interact with me and with their own children. I understood that the rest of my life would not have to be the same as it was at that moment in time. I could see that people could have normal, healthy, loving relationships. I could see that people could obtain various levels of success and abundance in their lives. I knew I wanted to be like them.

I'll never forget my uncle Jim, who unfortunately passed away much too soon. He dressed as Santa Claus when we were young, and he always greeted me with a powerful hug. Even when I was a teenager, he still insisted on giving hugs. He had such a strong, joyful laugh. When I was in the Single Independent Living Program, I lived only a few blocks away from his business and his house. He often invited me over for dinner. During the summer, the two of us would sit on his back porch and talk for hours. He understood what had happened in my life, and he wanted so much more for me. He'd always try to convince me to stay out of trouble and take control of my life. Uncle Jim lent me the money to buy my first car. I wasn't sure how I'd repay him, but he trusted me, which meant so much. I did pay him back, even if it was only twenty-five or fifty dollars at a time. He helped me see that I could create more out of life than what I had experienced up until that point. He taught me not to accept the bad but to create good. I miss him.

As a child, I always loved visits to my grandmother's house. Almost every weekend visit with Michael included a visit to Grandma's house. She was proud of all her grandchildren, and all she ever wanted was for her family to be together, healthy and happy. She created a family where all the aunts, uncles, and cousins got together for all holidays and special events. They put together amazing feasts on Christmas and Thanksgiving. She planned picnics and birthday celebrations in the parks. Because I lived with Frank and Sharon, I wasn't able to attend all these celebrations, but when I did, I was on top of the world. Being able to play with my cousins and enjoy good food gave me moments in time where I could forget about everything else and just enjoy being a kid. My uncles taught me to play cribbage and horseshoes. Good memories, good times.

Even when I was a teenager getting into trouble, Grandma continued to display her unconditional love for me. She always kept her door open for me when I had no place to live. On a few occasions, I stayed with her for short periods. She wanted her family together so badly that during the times I lived with her, she'd always invite Michael over for dinner in the hopes that we could work things out. Unfortunately, those dinners always ended up with one of us storming out of the house. I hated to see her cry, so I knew I couldn't stay there. Even though I chose not to live with her, my relationship with her was always extremely important to me. I went over almost weekly for coffee or lunch visits. Grandma Beverley taught me the power of love.

Immediate or extended family members can turn out to be some of our greatest assets. Maybe we can find comfort in their love, encouragement, or even in something as simple as sharing a laugh with them. You may not be comfortable sharing your entire story with them, but perhaps just their presence, the time you spend with them, will give you strength and hope. Connect with these people if and when you can. You may find more help than you knew was there.

> **Resiliency builder**: Who in your extended family could you spend more time with? Who boosts you up? Who provides an example of love or success that you want to emulate? And how can you spend more time with them this month?

I once heard in a lecture that friends were God's way of apologizing for the family he gave you. Of course, this is merely a joke, but there is truth in the significance friendship plays in our lives. Who else knows us better than our closest friends? When no one else seems to understand us, our friends are often the only people on whom we can lean. The bonds that we create with these people can be so incredibly powerful and in some cases withstand the tests of time. Some friendships will be formed during different stages of your life and then begin to deteriorate when they no longer serve a purpose for one or both people involved. The two people who once shared the same path find themselves on completely different journeys, heading out in different directions. Whether the friendship is short term or long term, each one serves a purpose. The purpose may be for us to experience ourselves, who we truly are, through the experiences and interactions we share with our friend. The purpose may be for safety and comfort or joy and pleasure. It can be a common goal or interest that brings you together. Our friendships can help us get through the toughest times in our lives and help us celebrate the best times. This probably makes sense to you if you've experienced true friendship, but if you haven't, you might be having a hard time relating.

Sometimes we find ourselves in "perceived friendships." These aren't friendships at all; they are only people with whom we happen to be spending time. These friendships lack meaning. If the relationship is one that encourages you to harm yourself or others, makes you feel belittled, or puts you in situations you don't want to be in, it's probably not a true friendship. If this sounds like relationships that you are in, you probably should reevaluate the need to continue these relationships.

True friendships are those that empower us with strength, hope, and joy. An authentic friendship never makes us feel bad about who we are or mistakes we have made. In these relationships, there is genuine concern for the well-being of one another. There is a willingness to do whatever is in our power to help that person in times of need.

Throughout my childhood, I typically attracted the same types of friends over and over again. These friends were usually children from abusive or neglectful families. In many ways, we shared the same mind-sets of being angry at the world for our childhood experiences. Our collective mind-set created even more chaos in our lives as we took part in breaking the law and using drugs and alcohol. These relationships did serve a purpose in my life, as I did experience myself through and with these people, many of whom were good-hearted, well-intentioned beings. Looking back, I think some of us just felt lost and helpless. But I grew tired of feeling lost.

When I began taking responsibility for my own life, the majority of these perceived friendships disintegrated.

After high school, I met Ron. Upon meeting, we discovered that we had both traveled similar paths, right from our childhoods up until that moment we met. To respect his privacy, I won't share any more of his story than that. Ron and I immediately connected because we both shared a common goal. We both wanted a better life for ourselves and for our own children than what we had experienced. We had both chosen to "break the cycles," as discussed in the previous chapter. We got jobs together, working for the same companies; we became roommates; and we even started a painting company together, which he now operates on his own. We created our new lives together, and as each of us took our stumbles along the way, the other was there to catch him. As we experienced new adversities in our lives, the other was there for support and encouragement. Ron has been my best friend for over ten years now, and I am thankful to have been able to share so much of this journey with him.

Friends, family, teachers, neighbors, coaches, and those in the helping professions can all be critical components in helping us triumph over adversity. We simply cannot do it on our own. We must identify those people in our lives with whom we can connect. You do not have to share your entire story with each of these people, as the relationship itself may be enough to give you strength, bring you hope, or get you through a particular experience. Identifying and connecting with supports helps us address the "I HAVE" component of resiliency. I have people around me that I can trust and who love me. I have people who will help me. I have people who will protect me. I know that for some of you, this may seem like an almost impossible thing to achieve. You may feel so alone - with no supports at all. I want you to look closely at all the people in your life. Look at your school, your community, and the different organizations and support services available. They are there, but we need to be the ones who reach out.

Understand and accept that not all relationships will last a lifetime. You will attract some people into your life for only brief moments of time. You will leave some people, and some people will leave you through death or simply because the relationship has served its purpose and no longer needs to exist. Try to appreciate that the end of a relationship is not always a bad or terrible thing. Sometimes the space that is left from the absence of one person is required for the next experience of your life to unfold ... or for the next person to enter.

However, try not to approach relationships from a view of what you will or can get out of a relationship. It should never be about "What's in it for me?" Instead, it

> **Resiliency builder**: Think of a relationship from your past that caused you a lot of pain and grief. Would you want to be in this type of relationship again? What do you need to do to ensure you don't attract this same experience again?

should be "What can I or did I learn about myself through this/that relationship?" This is particularly true when relationships end. If we spend our energy trying to figure out why this person has come in or out of our lives instead of asking ourselves what we learned about ourselves and our world through that relationship, we run the risk of repeating it over and over again. This means you will likely continue to attract the same types of people and relationships into your life. Now, if you typically attract positive and joyful relationships into your life, then it's not a bad thing. But if you typically attract abusive, harmful, or painful experiences/relationships into your life, you may want to learn the lesson and avoid repeating the experience again.

Before I close this chapter, I would like to speak to all of you who play roles in children's lives. This encompasses such a large, diverse group of people who extend beyond but include teachers, parents, foster parents, coaches, instructors, uncles, aunts, grandparents, neighbors, social workers, doctors, etc. Know that even the smallest gestures can have the biggest impact on a child's life. Taking the time to recognize and acknowledge a child's strengths, abilities, gifts, and talents has an incredible effect on a child's well-being. We all need to be accountable for the health and wellness of all the children in the world. If we continue to increase our energy in working together, we can begin to see more happy endings and happy beginnings. Together, we can create even more ripples. Each moment you spend with a child could be the one that really matters.

It is a pivotal and beautiful moment in a child's life when they connect with an adult and feel that someone really 'sees' them for the first time. Most of us have been fortunate enough to have had that experience as children. Many years later, as adults, we are still able to reflect back to that moment – remembering the person who changed our story for the better. Sometimes we take the time to share with that person the difference they made in our life, but so often, they are never told. Despite not always seeing the immediate effects of our work with children, when we open our hearts, there is no doubt that we touch theirs. With just a small gesture of kindness, quality time spent together, or a demonstration of compassion, we all hold the ability to be that light in a child's life.

I remember clearly and with profound gratitude those moments in my life. They came to me through the support of wonderful teachers, counselors, and members of my extended family that opened my eyes to my true potential. Those people likely didn't realize at the time the impact they were having on shaping my future. At the moment when they reached out to look beyond the surface of what they saw in me was the moment that they created an amazing ripple that has since then extended beautifully in all directions.

CHAPTER 8 –
Identify the World You Live In

Quantum physicist Albert Einstein is known for his brilliant scientific mind. You may know him for his theory of relativity. Albert Einstein was also a spiritual being who was very connected to the universe. He said that the most fundamentally important question we can ask ourselves is, "Do I live in a hostile or a friendly universe?" Take a moment and answer that question for yourself.

He went on to say that "no matter what your answer is to the question, you are correct."

Successful entrepreneur Henry Ford had a similar quote: "Whether you think you can or think you can't, either way you are right."

What do these two historical figures have in common? The answer is that they both understood the law of attraction. We all understand the law of gravity, right? What goes up must come down. It's a simple concept. Well, the law of attraction is similar in that it is a universal law that works every time for everyone. The theory is also quite simple: like attracts like.

Rhonda Byrne gave the world a beautiful gift when she released *The Secret*. *The Secret* is a movie and a book that teaches us how to use the power of the law of attraction to create the life we desire.

You see, our bodies are like transmitters, and our thoughts are the frequencies we send out to the universe. Scientifically, thoughts can actually be measured by their frequencies. Whatever frequencies we send out, we attract more of the same back into our lives. Think back to Dr. Einstein's question. Did you determine that you live in a hostile or a friendly universe? If you think that the world you live in is an unfriendly place where the world is out to get you, where it is full of pain, sadness, and upset, then I guarantee that you will continue to get even more experiences full of pain, sadness, and upset. It is only once we begin to shift our thoughts that we can begin to create the life we desire.

I have had this conversation with dozens and dozens of individuals, and each person has a strong position on this theory. Some see it as the only way to live their lives and incorporate it as daily practice. Others are skeptical and are not open to this concept at all. I didn't believe it either . . . at first.

After I escaped my childhood adversities, I found I was still confronted with many new challenges. They were just different challenges. I struggled with my finances and could never seem to get ahead of the debt I was accumulating. I struggled with my intimate relationships, always finding reasons to sabotage them. The adversities continued to flow into my life.

When I was introduced to a video of Dr. Wayne Dyer, *The Power of Intention*, I learned about the law of attraction. My life began to change . . . again. In his presentation, Dr. Dyer talks about how "the moment we begin to change the way we look at things, the things we look at will change." He understood this universal law. He knew that if we continued to focus on all the debt in our lives, we would simply accumulate more debt. The more energy we spend being unhappy, the more unhappiness we will attract. His message is to stop focusing on what you don't want to manifest in your life and begin creating intentions on what you do want in your life. When you begin to shift your thoughts like this, you will begin spending less time worrying about what you don't want, and thus the things you look at will change.

This is such a critical concept of the law of attraction. *The Secret* teaches us that the first step in attracting what you want is to ask for it. You literally place your order with the universe and begin attracting what it is that you want: money, happiness, relationships, your dream job . . . the list can go on, with no limits whatsoever. I can't disclose all of *The Secret* to you. For that, you'll need to read the book or watch the movie, but what I can tell you is that the universe cannot decipher between what you really want and what you really don't want. The problem with human beings is that we often spend more time worrying about what we don't want in our lives instead of thinking about what we do want. The universe responds by giving us whatever it is that we are thinking about and feeling about the most.

Remember, like energy attracts more like energy. Therefore, even if what you truly want is to find companionship, abundance, feel loved, and so on, if you spend most of your energy on feeling alone, seeing the shortages in your life, or fears of being rejected, that is exactly what the universe will provide you.

The more adversity you have experienced in your life, the harder this exercise may be for you, but don't let that stop you from trying it. If all or most of your life has been full of pain, sadness, disappointment, and fear, then it is understandable that you would think the world is full of pain, sadness, disappointment, and fear. Our past experiences often set the stage for what lies ahead, but you have just discovered a tool that you can use to change that. History does not need to repeat itself. We learned that from the "Breaking the Cycles" chapter.

Even after I realized I had overcome the adversities of my childhood, I still had not found the happiness that I sought. I felt as if I had been robbed of my childhood. I was so angry with the people from my past. My mind continually created thoughts of revenge, hatred, and sadness. I felt sorry for myself and all that I had endured. I'd fall in and out of depression for years to come. Life became a constant struggle. I wanted to find peace, love, and happiness, but my thoughts were rarely focused on peace, love, or happiness. Instead, my energy was spent on feeling alone and helpless. In Dr. Dyer's *Power of Intention*, he teaches us that no amount of feeling bad can bring about any good. "No amount of your defending not feeling good does anything to make yourself or anyone else feel good." We simply cannot feel bad enough to bring about any change in our lives. You can spend hours, days, or even months shedding tears and allowing pain to fester in your body, but you will never shed enough tears to change your situation or bring happiness to your life. It simply does not work. If feeling bad or feeling sad were the answer to our problems, I would be writing a book on the healing power of feeling bad. Any negative emotions we allow ourselves to experience will only bring more negative thoughts, feelings, and experiences into our lives.

Since I don't want the message to get misinterpreted, I feel the need to insert some clarification here. There are always exceptions to the rules, and the exception to this rule is if the pain and grief you are experiencing is fresh, meaning something has recently happened to you - new wounds, if you will. In situations where your pain is fresh, I believe you do need to be present and allow yourself to experience the loss, the pain, or any of the feelings and emotions that come to you. We need to experience and honor those feelings and emotions before we can move onto healing.

Now, this goes beyond positive thinking. Good thoughts are nice but still not powerful enough to bring about any significant change. We need to experience what we desire on an emotional level, through our feelings. We must totally shift our thoughts, and we can begin by letting go of our pasts. Childhood adversity is a terrible thing. A child should never have to endure the pain of being abused or neglected on any level. And yet this truth exists, and many of you reading this book are survivors of that adversity. How can we expect to bring about any change if we choose to carry these experiences, memories, and emotions into the unwritten chapters of our lives? We must reach a point where we say, "So what? Yes, I was abused . . . Yes, I was a drug addict . . . Yes, I was unwanted . . . Yes, I was violated. So What?"

I am not trying to belittle any experience. Each of these types of experiences *had* incredible pain. They only continue to *have* incredible pain through our allowing them to do

> **Resiliency builder**: Think of the top adversities you have been faced in your life. How much influence do these adversities have on your happiness or lack thereof? Are you ready to say, *So what - that happened to me*? Are you ready to see the world as a friendly place?

so. Try using *So what?* The real "what" is what are you going to do now.

Begin by identifying the world you live in as a friendly place. This may feel like a lie at first. Your outlook on life has been conditioned by your past experiences. We are no longer living in our pasts; we are only concerned with right now. Go beyond positive thinking and get to a place where you can feel the peace, love, and harmony that you desire. Feel it through your emotions. What would your life look like if you attracted the things, people, and experiences that you want? What would it feel like? Once you identify that feeling, don't let go of it. Re-create it in your mind over and over again as you visualize and begin to create the life you want. See yourself as the good that you desire.

You get to decide if you want to embrace the law of attraction or dismiss it. No matter which side of the fence you are on, I hope that you can appreciate that our thoughts and the way we perceive the world around us do have incredible power over what will unfold next in our lives.

Remember that you are the deliberate creator of your life. Regardless of how young or how old you think you might be, we all possess this power. Until you get used to living your life with this new outlook, you may get discouraged if you don't see immediate changes or results. Think of Henry Ford's quote: "Whether you think you can or think you can't, either way you are right." Once you see yourself having feelings of doubt or find yourself caught in your old ways of thinking, simply bring yourself back and remember that your life can be what you create it to be.

I have not yet fully mastered this law of attraction myself. I still get caught in fear and doubt at times, but as I continue to apply its basic principals into my everyday life, life continues to get better and better. I am able to attract the right people and experiences into my life which brings me closer to each intention that I've created for myself. My relationships and my finances have improved incredibly, and if this book finds itself in your hands, it is only another example of the power this law has. It is my intention that this book will become an international best seller and will find its way to those who need it the most.

The little boy who cried himself to sleep at night and stared up at the ceiling talking to God in Chapter 1, would fantasize about a better life until he fell asleep. I created a magical life in my mind; one without abuse, pain, and sadness. Even in my most magical fantasies, my life did not look half as wonderful, amazing or glorious as it is right now. I have created a life full of peace, love, and abundance. I have done that by seeing the world as a beautiful place and staying in a state of gratitude for everything and everyone who comes into my life.

Identifying the world you live in addresses the "I AM" and "I CAN" resilient components. I am confident that things will be all right. I am willing to be responsible for what I do. I can find healthy ways to solve problems.

Here is how powerful this law of attraction is. I have a 365-day calendar of *The Secret* that I keep in front of me on my desk. This morning before I began to write, I read today's message:

Tuesday May 13

If you go back over your life and focus on the difficulties from the past, you are just bringing more difficult circumstances to You now. Let it all go, no matter what it is. Do it for You. If you hold a grudge or blame someone for something in your past, you are only harming You. You are the only one who can create the life you deserve. As you deliberately focus on what you want, as you begin to radiate good feelings, the law of attraction will respond. All you have to do is make a start, and as you do, you will unleash the magic.

I couldn't have found a better way to introduce the next chapter.

CHAPTER 9 –
Forgiveness

In elementary school, we began each day by reciting The Lord's Prayer. "Our Father, who art in heaven . . . and forgive us our trespasses as we forgive those who trespass against us . . ." At that time in my life, the prayer held no meaning to me. It was just something coded to my memory. The concept of forgiveness was beyond me. What did it mean?

The Roman Catholic and Orthodox Christian churches teach that God's forgiveness is received through personal repentance in conjunction with the ministry of the church, that is, the body of Christ. In these churches and in some Anglican communities, it is customary to make formal confession of sins, usually in the presence of a priest. Most Protestant denominations teach that a believer receives forgiveness more directly through a sincere expression of repentance to God, and that the believer completes this in the act of forgiving others. In Buddhism, forgiveness is seen as a practice to prevent harmful thoughts from causing havoc on one's mental well-being. Some religious doctrine's philosophies place greater emphasis on the need for humans to find some sort of divine forgiveness for their own shortcomings, while others place greater emphasis on the need for humans to practice forgiveness between one another. Most world religions include teachings on the nature of forgiveness, but what does it truly mean to forgive someone?

I love asking that question to my audiences: "How many of you truly believe you have successfully forgiven someone from your past who has wronged you in some way or another?" A typical response involves around 20 percent of the people in the audience raising their hands. I don't ask the question because I want people to feel bad for not forgiving. I want to demonstrate the point that forgiveness is a hard concept to get your head around.

My adoption was never kept secret from me. As far back as I can remember, I knew I had been adopted. At first, I'd fantasize about my birth parents as being kind, gentle people, nothing like the parents I had been given. I thought that if they could only find out how difficult my life had become, they would come and find me and take me away. As life grew more and more difficult, and as I experienced more and more pain, my fantasies of these amazing people shifted to thoughts of anger and bitterness. How could they just give me away? I believed it was their fault I had such a terrible life. As I grew older, my resentment of their abandonment grew. People often asked me if I wanted to find my biological family, and my answer was always *No way*. I had enough so-called mothers and fathers in my life; I certainly did not need any further complications. In my mind, I would try to figure out the details of my adoption. Did my parents even love each other? Maybe my mother had been raped and couldn't bear having me around as a constant reminder. Regardless of what story I conjured up, I was always angriest with my father. I believed that a man was supposed to take care of his family and be responsible for them. *My* life was all *his* fault.

In my later teen years, the uncertainty of who I was began to burden me. I'd watch my friends interact with their parents and see the resemblances they had with one another. I wondered if I looked or sounded like somebody in my biological family. I wondered if I had any brothers or sisters.

My curiosity prompted me to begin looking for my family. The outcome was uncertain, and I still had no desire to establish relationships with these people, but I simply had too many unanswered questions. When I was nineteen years old, I registered with the Post Adoption Registry, the provincial government department where all adoption documentation is kept. Three weeks later, I received a reply in the mail. However, no one from my biological family had registered, so I only received non-identifying information. The three-page document provided me with some basic information about my parents, such as each one's ethnicity, height, build, hair, and eye color. My mother had two brothers and three sisters, and my father had two brothers and three sisters. It said that my biological parents had known each other for eight years. They had been married to each other but divorced before my birth. Aside from that, there wasn't anything of much interest – and definitely nothing that would help me find them. I shouldn't say there was nothing of interest. Two sentences that actually created much interest: "Our records indicate that you were the second child born to your birth mother. She had a son born four years before you who was in her care and custody."

I had a brother! I couldn't believe it. All this time, I had a brother. I wondered if he knew about me. I bet we looked identical. Suddenly, my interest in finding my family turned into a cause. I just had to meet my brother! I went to the public library and ordered three months of microfiche from the *Edmonton Journal*. I was born in Edmonton, Alberta, Canada, so I thought there could be a chance that a birth announcement had been placed in the newspaper. No such luck. I'd watch the reunion episodes of television talk shows and fantasize that one day I would be on *Oprah, The Montel Williams Show,* or The *Maury Povich Show* and get to meet my family. I registered with dozens of adoption websites, but all my efforts were unsuccessful.

Four years passed, and I had pretty much given up on my cause, as I was no closer to finding anyone. Right around my birthday in 1999, I woke up one morning, with an overpowering urge to phone the Post Adoption Registry. It truly came from nowhere. As I was talking to the gentleman who had my file, I began fabricating a lie. I told him that I had recently moved and somehow lost all the adoption documentation. In fact, I was holding all the documentation in my hand as I was speaking to him, but something told me to request the information again. A few weeks later, the documentation arrived in the mail. Everything was the same as before, with one tiny exception. There was a letter with my full biological name on it. For the first time in my life, I knew my birth name.

I went on the Internet and printed off pages of telephone directories of people who had the same last name as I. I began calling them one by one. I introduced myself with my full biological name, told them I was born in Edmonton, given up for adoption, and searching for my family. Many people were moved by my story, but no one knew of me. Call after call, the result was the same. I couldn't give up, though. Surely someone out there knew who I was, where I came from. On my twenty-sixth or twenty-seventh phone call, I spoke with an elderly woman. She was kind and gentle but had no idea who I was. She spoke of her late husband and mentioned his three sons and three daughters. According to the non-identifying information the Post Adoption Registry had sent me, my father had two brothers and three sisters. I asked her the names of the children and circled them on my lists of telephone directories as she listed them. I was so close, I could feel it.

My next phone call was so confusing and frustrating. I spoke to a woman named Wanda and gave her my rehearsed speech of who I was, where I came from, and what I was looking for. She kept questioning my date of birth. Each time I told her, she told me that I must be mistaken. She knew of an adoption but insisted that I had the wrong birth date and would not disclose any more information.

Frustrated but determined, I called the next name on the list. After introducing myself, he told me that his brother had given a child up for adoption and gave me his phone number. I knew that if I called this number, I'd be speaking to my father. I was faced with a dilemma. I was angry with my father. I wasn't looking for my father. Everything that happened in my life was his fault. Then panic set in. What if he had a new family and didn't want this door opened in his life? If I didn't call him, how would I find my brother? I had come too far to turn back now. I dialed the number. A man answered, and I delivered my last rehearsed introduction.

There was silence on the other end of the telephone, followed by the sound of crying. I had found my dad. We spoke for two hours, as we both had a lifetime of stories to share. He told me I also had a half sister from his second marriage, and then he gave me my brother's telephone number.

I eagerly called my brother's house, and his wife answered. She explained that he wasn't home and asked if she could take a message. I told her to tell him that his brother had called. She was clearly in shock, and I could hear by the excitement in her voice that she knew about me. She then gave me my mother's phone number and told me she would have my brother call me as soon as he got home.

My mother had been expecting my call. Wanda, the woman with whom I had spoken earlier, turned out to be my aunt. Wanda had called my mother and explained that this boy was looking for her, but that he had given the wrong birth date. Apparently, it used to be a common practice for social workers to change birth dates on adoption documentation. I don't know exactly why but I suspect it was to make finding the biological family more difficult. All my documentation stated that I was born four days after my real date of birth. It's no wonder Wanda had been skeptical. Nonetheless, here I was, speaking with my mother for the first time. She had a soft, beautiful voice but carried so much pain concerning my adoption. I'm sure that telling her about my childhood horrors didn't help matters much. She told me that I had yet another half brother and half sister from her second marriage. I went from being alone to having two brothers and two sisters in one night. I only lived about a five-hour drive away from her and three of my siblings, so we arranged for a visit two weeks later. That night, I did get to speak with my brother as well as my sister from my dad's second marriage. It was an incredible experience to connect with them.

The first person I met was my mother. Too nervous to drive, I had asked a friend to drop me off. I stood outside the door of my mother's apartment, my heart pounding so hard I could hear the beats in my eardrums. After a few deep breaths, I knocked on the door. As she opened the door, tears drifted from her eyes and rolled off her cheeks. She asked quietly if she could hug me. I hugged her back but didn't feel any tears coming on. I hadn't cried since I was sixteen years old and couldn't dig up any tears even if I'd wanted to. She was beautiful and petite with wavy black shoulder-length hair. I felt like a giant standing there as my head rested above hers, and I could feel her sobbing into my chest.

Her apartment was immaculately clean, with only a few pictures and books on display. We sat at the kitchen table looking at photo albums and talking all afternoon. It was wonderful to see pictures of my mother and my siblings growing up, but inside I was also resentful that I had missed all of those experiences. I smiled politely as I turned the pages of family vacations, first days of school, and new homes presenting themselves for the first time, but my heart sank a little deeper with each image. My mother explained that she and my father had split up before my birth, and she just didn't think that she could raise two children on her own.

We had made a plan to go over to my brother's house for supper, where I could meet my two brothers and my sister. As we walked up to my brother's door, my stomach was in knots, as I had wanted to meet him ever since I knew I had a brother. So many fantasies had gone through my mind over the years as to who he was, what he looked like. My hands were sweaty, and a slight presence of nausea vibrated through my body. I stood at the bottom of the three steps leading up to his door and waited for my mother to knock. When he opened the door, I was shocked. He didn't look anything like me. He was a little shorter than I am, a lot stockier, and his hair was thick and wavy, while I am tall and thin with poker-straight hair. I thought maybe I had the wrong family.

He hugged me, and I felt the connection in his embrace. He didn't look or sound like the fantasies I'd created in my head, but he was my brother. My friends used to tease me when playing pool or snooker, as I was the only person anyone had ever seen who rested the cue between the knuckles of my middle and ring finger. That is, until they met my brother, who also rests the cue between the knuckles of his middle and ring finger.

Meeting my family for the first time that evening was magical. We visited, shared stories, and took pictures, including my first family portrait. It ended up being my half brother who looked like me; we even had the exact same short, messy, spiky haircut with blond streaks. I met the coolest sister I could ever ask for, and my brother and his wife also have two children. I was suddenly an uncle to a wonderful niece and nephew. The family I had fantasized about having throughout my childhood was now assembled in my brother's living room. It was so surreal.

I didn't meet my biological dad for a few months after my initial contact. We had written each other a few letters, but he lived deep in the mountains, a more than twelve-hour drive from his place to mine. I had already decided that I did not want to have much of a relationship with this man. Having all these new siblings was more than enough for me. My track record with fathers was terrible; every male role model in my life was a complete let down. I wasn't about to give another man that opportunity. I did want to see and meet him, though, at least once. I'd planned a trip for the upcoming summer and decided to stay for three days. I've always loved British Columbia, and he and his wife lived on a beautiful acreage at the foot of a mountain. When the time arrived, I packed up the car and let my thoughts wander during the long drive.

He was a stocky man who shaved his head bald. He and I had the exact same voice and eyes. He was a kind, gentle, spiritual being. They lived a simple lifestyle, almost hippie-like. I was attracted to their lifestyle and liked them both a lot. So simple, so connected to the universe. They seemed sincere and honest. I was enjoying my visit with them but still did not intend to establish a relationship with this man. I had decided that it was nice finally to meet him, but I simply did not want to see him again.

The last day of my visit came, and we all enjoyed a wonderful breakfast outside. After breakfast, my father presented me with a beautiful wooden chest that he had made. Tears started running down his face as he began sharing some of the emotions he was feeling from our visit. I wasn't very good when it came to those types of situations. For years, I had fought my tears. Suddenly, I felt as if my body were going to explode. I began to cry harder than I had ever cried in my entire life. I began yelling at him with profanities and hatred. I told him that I blamed him for everything that had happened to me. I repeatedly shouted, "I hate you!"

I expected his reaction to be like all the other father figures in my life. I thought he would yell back and tell me off. Or maybe we'd even get into a physical fight. He didn't yell, though. He kept saying, "I know, I know." I began crying harder and yelling louder, and he kept saying, "I know, I know." He encouraged me to let everything out. He wrapped his arms around me and whispered, "I'm sorry, my son. I hope you can forgive me." I expected a fight, but this man was accepting responsibility. He was asking for my forgiveness. No one had done that before. How could I stay angry with a man who wouldn't give me any reasons to be angry with him? I cried until I simply could not cry anymore. I was emotionally and physically exhausted, and at the same time, a giant weight had been lifted off my shoulders. The anger and resentment I had carried for my father all those years were suddenly gone. I just looked at him and forgave him.

I now have an amazing relationship with my dad. He is literally the father I never had. I have come to know, respect, and love him very much. He helped me with my first lesson on the power of forgiveness. I forgave both my mother and my father. I hope this book puts to rest any doubts either of them may have. I know they both made the best decisions that they could under the circumstances they were in. No one could have foreseen the childhood I would have with adoptive parents. I know that their intentions were for me to have a better life than they could have provided. I have spent the last ten years catching up on lost time with my entire family. I am close to all my brothers and sisters. We enjoy visits and camping trips together and sometimes it feels as if we were never apart.

It can often be easier to forgive those who actually seek our forgiveness. When someone is truly sorry for any pain or grief that she or he may have caused you, our hearts can open up and accept the apology. That was the case with my birth father.

But what about those who have wronged us and are not looking for our forgiveness? What about those who may not know, believe, or admit to the pain they brought to our lives?

When I began my training and education to be a youth counselor, I started to understand the importance of letting go of the past. Part of my education was to examine my own life and see how I overcame my own adversities. One of my papers was to write a life history assignment. I remember writing about "Kyle's" story in that assignment and experiencing much of the pain that had been repressed for many years. I knew I had to get through it in order to allow the healing process to begin. Once the paper was completed, I felt that I had put to rest the troubles of my past. I knew that if I wanted to be a successful counselor, I had to let go of any anger and resentment I carried and declare forgiveness to those from my past, such as Frank and Michael.

So that is what I did. I sat at my desk in my living room and just decided to forgive everyone who had hurt me in any way. It was as if I were surrendering my anger and my pain over to the universe. I didn't talk to anyone; I didn't write anything down. Thinking about each person, I just thought *I forgive you.*

For the first time in my life, it felt as if things were unfolding the way I had intended. I'd graduated from college, received fantastic jobs working with children and families, found my biological family, and eventually started my company, Wellness Realization, speaking to youths and adults. Life was so good. My past was behind me, and my future was promising.

I was able to maintain this momentum for a few years. Then, all of a sudden, things seemed to stall. My professional speaking career seemed to plateau. My presentations of Kyle's story were still powerful, but I didn't feel I was leaving the audiences with much more than a sad story. I wasn't leaving them with enough tools and resources that they could apply to their own lives. My personal life was full of constant struggles. I was sabotaging every intimate relationship I was in. I went from one relationship to the next, thinking that it was always the person I was with who wasn't making me happy, but the next person I was with would. So many relationships suffered, and I was at a loss for why I was creating so much chaos in my own life. I definitely didn't want chaos in my life. I wanted to achieve success, inspire people, love people, and create a life with someone. Things weren't making any sense.

During a visit back in my hometown, my friends and I decided to go bowling one night. We were having a great time sharing laughs and stories when, out of the corner of my eye, I saw a familiar face. It was Frank. Remember Frank . . . my adoptive mom's second husband? I had only bumped into Frank three or four times since I'd moved out of his house at twelve years of age, and each of those instances had only lasted seconds or a few minutes at most. Now we were both in the same building and found ourselves staring at one another. I didn't know for sure if he actually recognized me, and yet neither of us broke the stare. My body became flushed with anger and intense heat. I could feel my fists clench, my heart race, and I began to fantasize about giving him a beating like he had given me so many times before. I was convinced that it was only a matter of seconds before I'd walk up to him and punch him in the face. I couldn't take it anymore, so I stood up and walked out.

As I arrived home, I hated the way I felt. I hated the fact that I could still be carrying so much anger inside me. I was so confused. I thought I had let all of this go. The pain and anger sat with me for days to follow. That week, I had attracted into my life one of the most powerful books I have ever read: *Left to Tell,* by Immaculee Ilibagiza. Immaculee is a genocide survivor whose entire family had been murdered during the Rwandan holocaust. As the rest of the world was focused on the O.J. Simpson trials, over one million people were murdered in roughly one hundred days. Immaculee came face-to-face with the people who murdered her family, people who wanted to murder her, and offered them her forgiveness.

I was in awe as I read Immaculee's story. My story and Immaculee's story cannot be compared on any level. I cannot even begin to imagine the pain she experienced. Yet what a beautiful gift she has given the world through her book - what a beautiful lesson. I knew what I had to do. I had to forgive Frank; I mean, *really* forgive him.

The next weekend I drove back to my hometown. On Saturday, I drove past Frank's house eight times but just could not find the strength to pull the car over. I was disappointed in myself for not following through but determined that I had to see him before I left town. Sunday, I drove past his house another eight times, and on the ninth time, I pulled over. He still lived in the same house that I had left when I was twelve. Not knowing what Frank's response would be, sweat began beading up on my forehead as I walked up the driveway. I began to question if I would be able to stay in a place of peace and love regardless of Frank's response to my visit.

Frank and Sharon were no longer together, and his new girlfriend responded to my knock. As I entered the house, I could see Frank sitting in the living room in the chair he had always sat in, right where I had imagined him to be. I told him that I needed to talk to him and asked him to come outside with me. He was friendly, and our conversation began almost as if we were two old friends who had not seen each other in years. I looked into his eyes and told him that I forgave him for all the times he had hit me as a child. I told him that I hoped he would find peace in his heart and love and happiness in his life. Then I left.

Eckhart Tolle's book *A New Earth* is a brilliant masterpiece that is touching the lives of millions of people all across the globe. In his book, Tolle says, "It requires honesty to see whether you still harbor grievances, whether there is someone in your life you have not completely forgiven, an "enemy." If you do, become aware of the grievance both on the level of thought as well as emotion, that is to say, be aware of the thoughts that keep it alive, and feel the emotion that is the body's response to those thoughts. Don't try to let go of the grievance. Trying to let go, to forgive does not work. Forgiveness happens naturally when you see that it has no purpose other than to strengthen a false sense of self, to keep the ego in place."

Eckhart's explanation of the forgiveness process explains why my previous efforts of letting go of my past did not work. My anger and my pain were serving me as a means of protection against potential adversity. When we endure enough adversity and enough pain in our lives, our bodies and our minds begin to develop defense mechanisms. We wear these defense mechanisms like an impenetrable coat of armor. We wear this armor or build solid walls around ourselves that distance us and protect us from the outside world. As we continue to experience adversity, these walls, or this armor, protect us and lessen the pain and hurt we endure. They protect us, give us strength, and serve us.

That sixteen-year-old boy, with the extension cord wrapped around his neck, who swore he'd never allow himself to get close to anyone ever again, kept his promise. I was determined to maintain a safe distance from any relationship so that I would not have to experience pain, disappointment, or letdown. The impenetrable armor that I created served me as I continued along in my journey, until one day it didn't any longer. Until I saw Frank in the bowling alley, until I began to look at my relationships with women, family and friends, and until I finally realized that this armor I wore to protect me was actually hurting me, I would be forever trapped in the endless cycle of negativity. It was preventing me from having meaningful relationships with anyone. It was even preventing my business from expanding, as I could not inspire and help others if I could not find inspiration and help for or within myself. It

> **Resiliency builder**: Are you ready to remove the body armor that has protected you for so long? Are you truly ready to let go of the pain, grief, and loss that once made you stronger? How does holding onto that pain continue to serve you?

no longer served a purpose. Once I finally realized this, I could lift the armor off my shoulders, tear down the walls brick by brick, and allow forgiveness and healing to begin.

I have forgiven Frank, Michael, Sharon, Lynne, and absolutely everyone from my past. Some I have forgiven in person. Some I have simply forgiven in my own space. There is no right or wrong way, no correct process you need to follow. You just need to decide that your ill feelings no longer serve you, and the process will just happen. I choose not to have a relationship with any of these people, but this choice is no longer based on anger or resentment. I am on my own journey, and they are on theirs. In this moment, our paths are not aligned. With sincerity, I hope they all find peace in their hearts, love in their lives, and unlimited abundance.

Love is forgiving or for giving.

We must examine one final type of forgiveness before we can close this chapter: the forgiveness of ourselves. I have but one regret in this life. I wish I had come to this point in my life without hurting so many people along the way. Those who tried to love me, tried to help me, I rejected or dismissed. The irony is that I may not have ever come to this place in my life without those experiences and those people. I hope that they will find forgiveness in their hearts for any pain I may have caused them.

Every free choice we make comes from a thought of love or a thought of fear. Sometimes our choices will bring others or ourselves pain. Our actions, behaviors, and words can be perceived as insult, disrespect, dishonoring, and cruelty. Intentional or not, we may be the reason for someone else's pain, anger, and adversities. We aren't often unaware of the injuries we have caused. This acknowledgement may bring about intense feelings of shame, embarrassment, guilt, regret, and even anger towards ourselves. During these times, we must refer back to Dr. Dyer's teachings of how we cannot feel bad enough to change things for one person in the world. You cannot get sad enough, feel guilty enough, or ashamed enough to reverse what you did or to make someone feel better. We must find the ability to forgive ourselves. No amount of self-punishment will empower you or the ones you have wronged. Forgiving ourselves cannot be used as some free ticket to hurt or mistreat anyone. Wherever possible, we need to correct our wrongs. Where possible, we must ask forgiveness from those we have wronged. Forgiveness will not always be given, maybe not right away, maybe not ever, and sometimes there may be no action we can take to fix our mistakes. Still, we must find forgiveness in our own hearts, as emotions such as shame and guilt simply cannot serve us.

Forgiveness is giving up all hope of a better past.

We cannot change history, we cannot change our pasts, but we can find peace in the moments we have right now. The ability to forgive others and ourselves addresses the "I CAN" component of resiliency. I can find peace in my life. I can let go of any negative emotions that burden me.

CHAPTER 10 –
Live an Inspired Life

Many times throughout our lives, we will find moments in time where it may feel it is impossible to escape our past and our pains. Maybe you are going through tremendous pain right now, or maybe you haven't fully resolved your past. Perhaps you keep encountering triggers that re-create the adversities you have endured. I believe it is for moments like these that God gave us inspiration. Inspiration is one of the most powerful tools we have, and it can provide us with hope, strength, and empowerment to triumph over adversity. The wonderful thing about inspiration is that it can be found almost anywhere and everywhere. It can be found in a piece of music, a book, a movie, a poem, in art, or in nature. The list is truly endless. Inspiration is one of those things that no one can take away from you. You can carry it in your mind and in your heart always.

What truly inspires you? What types of activities or experiences fill your heart and soul with joy, love, and peace? I ask these questions to the many youths and adults that I meet in my travels. Some find inspiration in reading books or poetry. Many find inspiration in music, listening to their favorite songs and artists. Many people have told me they find inspiration in sports, whether playing, competing, or watching others compete. Many of us find it in the beauty and tranquility that nature provides us. As a child in elementary school, I grew up in a neighborhood that was surrounded with numerous coulees and ravines. It was in those coulees and ravines that I found serenity. No matter how bad things got at home, I could always escape my pain by spending time in nature. I loved observing the animals, building forts, exploring the creeks, and creating adventures in my mind. All this brought me peace when I needed it most.

My love for nature has followed me throughout my life, and it still brings me the peace and serenity I desire. As I wrote the pages of this book, I looked out over the breathtaking landscape of the Rocky Mountains. Due to the nature of the work that I do, with many traveling demands, I live in the city. I knew that to write this book, I'd need to surround myself with what inspired me the most. I rented a cabin in southern British Columbia. I spent my mornings hiking, exploring the landscape, finding amazing places to meditate, and I returned to the cabin to write. It was a powerful experience, and I don't know if I could have written this book without this experience - at least not this exact book as it has unfolded.

Inspiration that inspires us to create is the most powerful form of inspiration that exists. It results in creative form that inspires others. Many of you reading this book, and many of those whom I have interviewed, channel the flow of inspiration and turn it into beautiful, wonderful, and powerful things. Some of you write poetry, short stories, or even books. Some play musical instruments or write songs. Many people draw, paint, or contrive other artistic creations. Some are inspired to sing or dance. I have spoken with people who love to cook or bake and design mouth-watering dishes. There are no limits as to what we can create through inspiration, and we have no idea of the significant impact the results of our inspired actions and creations will have on others. All our favorite songs, books, movies, and pieces of art came from a place of inspiration, and I'd venture to guess that the composers, writers, and artists had little or no concept of the impact they would have throughout the world as they began to create. I encourage you to share your hidden skills and talents with the world. You may very well be holding the piece of inspiration that someone else is seeking. The book that you are now holding is a result of the many letters and emails I have received over the years from young people who came right out and told me that I should write a book. Others simply had more questions and were seeking answers. I have been inspired by you, and I hope that this book will inspire others.

Our passions, interests, and hobbies are all forms of inspiration. They are what give us hope, bring us joy, or at the very least, provide us temporary distractions from our adversities until we have the strength, will, or resources to take on our adversities. Live an inspired life. Surround yourself with the people, activities, and experiences that provide you with the most inspiration, and do these things as often as you can. The more adversity you have in your life, the more you will need these moments of inspiration to "recharge" your battery. Adversity, and even getting caught in the fast pace and high demands of life, can drain us emotionally and physically. The more drained we become, the more susceptible we are to poor health, lower energy, and lower frequencies of thoughts and feelings. Therefore, it is likely we will attract even more of this lower vibrating energy into our lives. When we come from a place of inspiration or act out of inspiration, we are vibrating at the highest frequencies possible. It is simply impossible to attract negative energy when you are in this state.

A few years ago, I received a phone call from a community who requested a presentation on cultural leadership. This particular community had an extremely diverse population, with people from all across the globe taking up residence there because of the employment opportunities. A small, rural community, that was unprepared for the challenges this quick, diverse growth would bring. Hate crimes, discrimination, and other related offenses were reoccurring problems faced by the community. The community responded by coordinating and hosting a cultural leadership conference and inviting people from all different cultures and ethnic backgrounds to attend. They asked me to be the keynote speaker. I was honored by their request but concerned that I might not be the right man for the job. I had done many presentations on leadership before but nothing with a cultural component. I was determined to put together the most powerful presentation that I could possibly conjure up. To do that, I needed to find inspiration.

Ever since I was a young boy, music has inspired me. So many songs have helped me get through some of the toughest periods. The brilliant lyrics and the synchronized tones and melodies of the instruments can take us away to other worlds. In my mind, it is one of the most brilliant means of storytelling we have.

I was telling a dear friend of mine about the upcoming presentation, and she told me about an amazing choir she had recently seen perform. She handed me their CD, which she had purchased at the event. She told me that I might find inspiration in their music. The CD was the African Children's Choir. My friend was right. As I listened to the CD, the harmony of these children's voices moved me. I went to the Internet to find out more about this choir. Their website began to inspire me even more (visit my website for the link). The choir consists of thirty children ages twelve to fifteen. Each child in the choir had lost one or both of his or her parents to poverty or HIV. Many of them had no food and nowhere to live, but through the wonderful organization called Music for Life, these children were given a place to live, an education, and an opportunity to triumph over adversity through the magic of song and music. Each year, a new choir is formed, made up of these children. They tour the world. All the money they raise goes back to Africa and is used so other children can have homes and receive an education.

As I continued listening to their CD, I was flooded with inspiration. As a hobby, I enjoy putting together slideshow-type videos, setting music to pictures of family and friends. I find perfect songs that capture the essence of the pictures, and on my computer, I can edit all this into a DVD. I thought putting together one of these videos would be a perfect way to close my cultural leadership presentation. I selected one of the African Children's Choir songs and began searching the Internet to find the perfect images of unity, love, and peace to flow with the music. I typically only put these types of videos together for family and friends or for myself to create wonderful memories of a vacation or trip I have taken. These videos always take me days, sometimes even weeks, to put together. This particular night, though, everything flowed so quickly, so naturally and so effortlessly.

I instantly found the right picture to accompany each part of the song. What normally would take days or weeks unfolded in six hours. I was so inspired, so in spirit, that I could feel the universe working with me in creating this video. It was so powerful, and I was so excited to think all of the participants at the cultural leadership conference would see this video. It was two o'clock in the morning, and my energy level was so high that I couldn't possibly think about sleeping. Suddenly, it hit me. I couldn't just use this video in my cultural leadership presentation. I had to give it to the African Children's Choir as a gift.

I went back to their website and looked at their touring dates. Sure enough, they were going to be performing in my community in two weeks. I contacted the church where they would be performing and explained that I had this gift for the children. The church asked me to come by so that they could view the video. Upon seeing it, they agreed that the video was something that had to be given to the choir.

The day came for me to meet these beautiful young people. I asked them if they had a music video. They looked at me in confusion and said no. I said, "Well, you do now," and I presented them with the video. They were so receptive and appreciative of my act of kindness. The children called me "uncle" and many of them held my hands as they led me around, introducing me to the family and friends that toured with them. There was such a love and connectedness in that room, so much more than I had ever experienced before.

My small act of kindness was indeed that, a small gesture that had flowed to me and through me from inspiration. Through this small act of kindness, I was able to have

> **Resiliency builder**: What is one thing that you could do today that would inspire someone else? It doesn't have to cost money. It doesn't have to be *HUGE*. It just has to come from a space of inspiration and kindness. Don't just identify it - *do* it!

one of the most powerful, rewarding experiences of my entire life. When you do something out of love, not for money or recognition but simply out of love, compassion, or kindness, you will encounter experiences that will fill your heart and possibly change your life forever. My experience with the African Children's Choir was truly priceless. I could not have created it through any other means but love. I was inspired by and continue to be inspired by the children in the choir and their ability to overcome incredible adversity. Their performances are full of genuine joy, love, and happiness. They have found peace with their adversities, hope and belief in a better future, and a purpose in using their gifts and talents to help and inspire others.

The cultural leadership conference was a tremendous success, as was the video I created. The organizing committee put together a powerful event that brought people together. The video inspired by the African Children's Choir was a big hit at the conference. Many had requested copies for themselves. The video was created out of inspiration and, in turn, has been inspiring people all over the world, as I show it at almost all of my public performances. I have not and will not ever charge money for the video, but I have posted the video on my website as a free download for anyone who wishes to see it. You can find it at www.wellnessrealization.net .

Another thing that you will find on the site is a list of what inspires me now. And there is a spot for you, the reader, to share your own inspiration. There are fields where you can submit the links for songs, videos, or websites that inspire you so that we can all share in each other's inspiration. I encourage you to participate and check it out.

Live an inspired life. Regardless of how bad things were or are right now, we can change the "right now" by incorporating inspiration into our lives. Inspiration will engage us to take positive action and will also attract more "like energy" to it. Living an inspired life addresses the "I CAN" component of resiliency. I can create peace and harmony in my own life. I can find healthy ways to make me feel good.

CHAPTER 11 –
Closing This Chapter in Life

This book is a true story. I have changed the names of those who appear in the book to protect their identity and their privacy. I know that some of the people mentioned may experience pain from the memories and experiences outlined herein. That is not my intention. I believe that we are all connected, that we are meant to learn from one another's experiences. I wrote this book hoping that others may find healing from Kyle's story . . . my story.

My story is told from my perspective, as I remember it. Our realities are only our perspectives of our experiences. Two people can share the exact same experience and yet have two completely different perspectives of that experience. Sharon denied my abuse for years, and even Frank, during the moment I forgave him, denied ever abusing me. Although I was convinced that my higher power was guiding me and telling me that I needed to forgive Frank, I was so confused. To have him deny the past just didn't make sense to me. At first, I started to become angry that he could dismiss our history together, but as I looked into his eyes, I could see that he truly believed that he had never wronged me and that his acts were no more than discipline. I realized that I didn't need to forgive Frank for the sake of Frank. I needed to forgive Frank for myself. He may never share my perspective of those moments in time, nor does he have to.

I wanted to ensure accuracy of the events I was to write about, so I obtained my child welfare file. Any child who has ever been involved with Child Protection Services or Child Welfare has a file created for all the documentation of those investigations. You have a right to your file and can obtain a copy of it once you are eighteen years of age. You need only to pay the costs of photocopying. In preparation for this book, I reviewed my file. The majority of it was pretty much as I had remembered, but it was interesting to see the perspectives of the numerous social workers and child protection workers involved. The investigations were dated as early as when I was four. I extend my appreciation to those who worked at helping me and those who work helping all youths in need. I know your jobs are not easy, and I know that your combined efforts are creating a multitude of ripples. On behalf of all children in protective custody, I thank you.

In preparation for this book, I also dug up my old life history assignment from college. As I read it, I couldn't believe how much my own perspective has changed. The man who wrote that assignment and the man who wrote this book are in some ways two totally different people. Even though I had grown and matured in giant leaps during the time I wrote that assignment, there was still much anger and pain hidden in the story. Chances are, you will have similar experiences. As we forgive, let go, and acquire peace in our lives, our perspectives of past experiences will change. The energy that our memories contain can be so incredibly powerful. It's when we stop giving energy to those memories that we truly begin to create the life we desire.

The tools I have outlined in this book are not new, nor are they my creations. Through my own healing, I have looked to the teachings and wisdom of spiritual mentors such as Dr. Wayne Dyer, Rhonda Byrne, Neale Donald Walsch, Eckhart Tolle, Joe Vitale, and countless others. I have applied and incorporated their teachings and principles into my own life and have created a life that I only dreamt about as a child. As these teachings and ideas are presented to you, they can be so inspirational. Simply reading or hearing these positive messages can begin to change your life, but the real power comes from the implementation. Opening your mind and being receptive is the first step, but applying the ideas outlined in this book is also necessary for you to see the real change unfold.

Remember, you are the one in control of the outcome. You are the one writing your own life's story. Keep in mind that breaking the behaviors and beliefs that have been engrained in you all of your life can be difficult. Our fears and our egos are powerful forces often working against our wills to break free of the cycles and chains that hold us down. I have spoken with many people who began applying these teachings but who became frustrated when they did not see immediate results or changes. Healing is a process and a journey in itself, and it can only take place when we surrender our self-limiting beliefs and come from a place of love. Love for ourselves and love for others.

We don't learn from experiences. We learn from reflecting on those experiences, which is why many of us repeat and attract the same types of experiences over and over, going from one bad relationship to another, going from one bad job to the next. It is almost like a do over until you get it right. Aren't we lucky? Except sometimes we don't want to relive the same experiences over. Taking time to reflect on our life experiences can change our course. We don't need to get bogged down in our pasts, but before we repeat them, we should take a moment for reflection and clarity.

The theories and concepts of resiliency have only been promoted since the mid-1990s and are thanks to the hard work of people like Dr. Edith Grotberg. As survivors of adversity, we need to incorporate these teachings into our own lives for healing. As parents or those in the helping professions, we must incorporate these teachings to the children of this generation and of the generations to come, ensuring our children develop "I AMs," "I CANs," and "I HAVEs." So many children in the system and in the world cannot confidently say any of those statements. It breaks my heart when children do not believe that they are good, do not believe there is anyone in their lives who loves them, and do not believe that things will be all right. Surely, as members of this universal community, we can step up and show them that someone does believe.

Remember, adversity excludes no one. Sometimes people feel that they are the only ones experiencing the adversity and pain they are currently in. You are not alone. The good news is that each day, more and more people are experiencing more happy endings or happy beginnings. For some of us, it just takes longer to get there. As a child, I tried to numb my pain with alcohol, drugs, and anger. These activities were only a way of temporarily distracting me from my pain, my fears, and my experiences. The behaviors I indulged in to numb my pain only created more pain in my life. It wasn't until I began working through the tools I outlined in this book that life began to fall into place. Soon I didn't need the distractions. Soon I could see this world as a friendly place.

I do not claim to be some perfect being who has all of the answers. I simply live and share my own experiences, hoping that others will benefit. My journey of healing and growth is not over but the peace in my heart and my gratitude for all of life's experiences has made the path bearable. In fact, they have made the path beautiful; for each experience, even the adversities, show me who I really am. I like who I am. I will love as much as I can from where I am. I will continue my journey of healing and spiritual growth, and I will create as many ripples as I can along the way.

The adversities in our lives have given us scars - some that are emotional and some of us even carry physical scars that can be seen. Our scars remind us where we've come from. They don't have to determine where we're going.

Peace, Love & Light to you all,,,

LaVergne, TN USA
03 March 2011
218599LV00001B/5/P